There's No I in Improv

The Complete Guide To The GS IMPROV
Technique With Over 50 Improv Games
Fully Explained

GREG SULLIVAN

Tp

Tunguska Press
Mount Kisco, New York

Copyright © MMX Greg Sullivan

Tunguska Press, Publisher
PO Box 721
Mount Kisco, New York 10549

Editor and Cover Illustrator: Sally Weisbard

Printed in the United States of America
First Edition

Any trademarks contained herein are the exclusive property of their companies.

All rights reserved. No part of this publication may be reproduced, stored in a retrieval system, or transmitted in any form or by any means, electronic, mechanical, photocopying, recording, or otherwise, without permission of the publishers.

The author and publisher disclaim liability arising either directly or indirectly from the use and application of this book. Regarding copyright permissions, any omissions or errors are unintentional and the publisher will, when notified, correct them in future printings.

ISBN 978-0-578-06641-7

For Sally and Emily Kate

Improv Is Easy Until You Know What You're Doing.

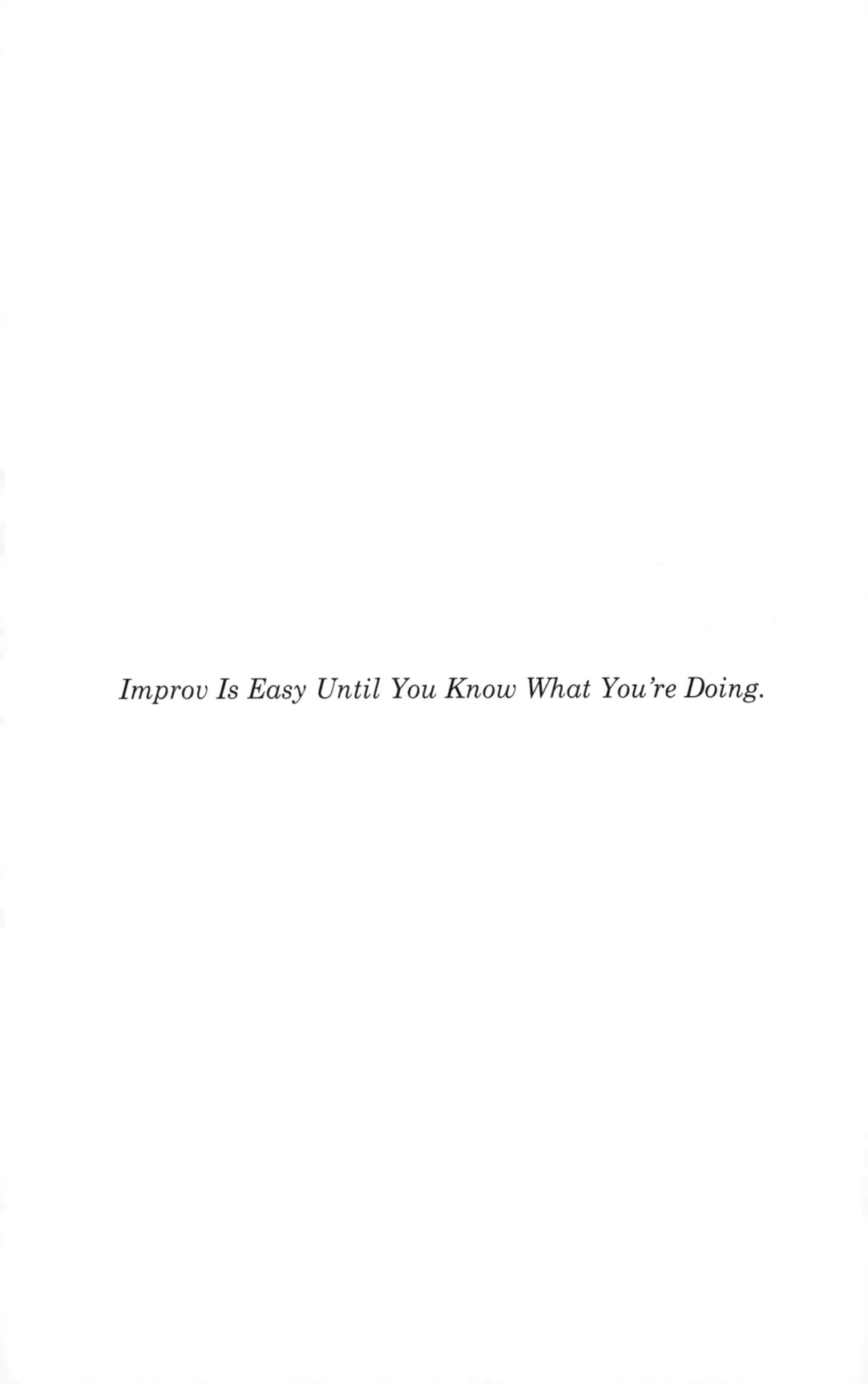

TABLE OF CONTENTS

PREFACE 1
INTRODUCTION 2
QUICK START GUIDE 7
THE GS IMPROV TECHNIQUE 11
   ESTABLISHING WHO THE CHARACTERS ARE 12
      USING THE FOURTH WALL EFFECTIVELY 16
   ESTABLISHING WHAT IS GOING ON 18
      BEING SPECIFIC 22
   RECAPPING THE THREE W's 23
   STARTING AN IMPROVISATION 23
   MAKING ALL OBJECTS IMAGINARY 28
   EMBRACING THE ACTOR/CHARACTER DUALITY 32
   ENTERING A SCENE 36
   TAKING FOCUS 37
   SEIZING THE SEMINAL MOMENT 41
   BEING FLEXIBLE 44

1. DRAW THE BLANK SPACE 47
2. TOE TOUCH YAAAAAAH 49
3. ARMS 1-10 50
4. MIRROR IMAGE 52
5. MOTION CHANGE 54
6. PASSING THE CLAP 56
7. SOCK TOSS 59
8. COUNTING 1 TO 10 62
9. CIRCLE EXERCISES 64
10. RHYMING COUPLETS 73
11. SLAP CLAP SNAP SPEAK 75
12. TOSS CHALLENGE 79
13. LIMERICKS 82
14. DA DOO RON RON 86
15. QUESTIONS ONLY 89
16. ENEMY/PROTECTOR 91
17. PASS THE BUCK 92

18. BIPPITTY BIPPITTY BOP 95
19. MAL OCCHIO 98
20. GREETING/RESPONSE 99
21. GOING AND TAKING 101
22. WHATCHA DOING 103
23. TWO CHAIRS 105
24. NUCLEAR CHICKEN 107
25. MAY I 108
26. FREEZE TAG 110
27. I'M THINKING OF A WORD 113
28. CELL PHONE 116
29. THREE SENTENCES 120
30. THREE PART JOKE 123
31. YOU DO, I DO 125
32. REPAIR SHOP 129
33. TWO AND ONE 131
34. EVERY SECOND COUNTS 137
35. WHAT'S GOING ON? 139
36. MYSTERY GUEST 141
37. JOB INTERVIEW 146
38. CLICHÉ 148
39. 1 TO 5 TO 1 151
40. THE HAROLD 157
41. HUMAN ORCHESTRA 162
42. A TO Z 90 172
43. DATING GAME 177
44. SIXTY SECONDS 190
45. POET'S CORNER 197
46. SEVEN-MINUTE STORY 203
47. SUPERHERO EULOGY 210

48. FIRST-LINE, LAST-LINE, WITH CHANGES 216
49. SPIN ROTATION 229
50. ULTIMATE JEOPARDY! 241
51. WRITTEN WORD 251
52. STRIP CHARADES 257
APPENDIX A: RECOMMENDED READING AND VIEWING
.... 268
APPENDIX B: FINDING THE RIGHT CLASS 272

PREFACE

Last I checked you actually do need the letter "i" to spell "improv." So what's the deal with the title? First, don't take everything in this book as Gospel. This book offers improv guidance and encouragement. In improv, as in life, find out what works for you.

Second, the mantra of improv is that it's a team-oriented game. So don't think in terms of "I." Think in terms of "we." Do you want to look good while you are performing? Then help the other performers look good. The lessons in this book will help you achieve that goal. There's no denying that there are players with different levels of skills. Some people are born naturals at improv. They instinctively know the correct action or line of dialogue at almost any given moment. Some of these highly skilled players just cannot help but have the spotlight come their way during a performance. Still, it is the best of the best who know how to work as teammates. Call it the NBA effect. Teams win when the best players defer their talents for the overall good of the team. That's what you want to strive for. As Mr. Spock once said, "it is not logical but it is often true."

INTRODUCTION

Improv is fun.

Improv is so much fun that you will remember the key moments of a well done improv many years after the fact. You can be young or old, tall or short, even Republican or Democrat – but not Whig – and have the same shot at being good at improv as anyone else. A well run improv class welcomes inexperienced, new-to-it-all students and those crusty, veteran, think-they-know-it-all improvisers. A good class makes room for everyone, because there's always room for talent, whatever stage it's in.

Improv is an important skill for actors. Professional performers know there is plenty of talent out there, just a shortage of opportunity. When you are an accomplished actor you can be frustrated by the inability to find work – whether it's landing the lead role you know you're perfect for, or any role at all. Improv is your chance to play the hero, the villain, the loser and the winner – and all in the same night!

Improv has its roots in the passion plays and Commedia dell'Arte of Italy during the Middle Ages, in which a group of characters would play out the same story each time but without a script – they would improvise. Much of contemporary improv training was developed by Viola Spolin in the 1930s and '40s and is recorded in her seminal work *Improvisation for the Theater*. A significant moment in improv history came in the 1950s when the Compass Players troupe was formed by University of Chicago alums, which led directly to the formation of The Second City in Chicago. (Treat yourself to a copy of *The Second City* by Sheldon Patinkin, if only to listen to the accompanying CD's "Wicked" with Tina Fey and Rachel Dratch.) Today there are many great schools where improvisation is taught. In addition to Chicago's Second City, there is The Groundlings in Los Angeles, and HB Studio, the Upright Citizen's Brigade and, naturally, GS IMPROV in New York City. (The Groundlings were the people who in Shakespearean times attended performances at theaters like the Globe and stood to watch. They were on the ground level – hence groundlings – and it was the moneyed classes who could afford seats, which were up in the balcony.) The BBC television show *Whose Line Is It, Anyway?* along with the fine American version hosted by the underappreciated Drew Carey, further helped familiarize audiences with what improv is about.

Improv is the best. It is a great way to express oneself creatively. It is an excellent way to show just how clever you are. It is a wonderful way to get out of the work-week grind. For actors, it's an imperative skill for their career because it teaches them to really listen to the other actors they are working with. In his book, *Making Movies*, the legendary director Sidney Lumet writes that the reason that actors of such diverse techniques can work well together is that on a very basic level they truly listen to one another. Lumet's book is not some tossed-off gossipy mess, but an important text for all aspiring actors to read. Even for us regular Joe-the-plumbers working 9-5 jobs, improv is great training for getting into the habit of really listening to people. You will find that better listening will lead to your responding to people quicker and with greater confidence.

When you take an improv class you get to spend time with special friends. You get to do something which helps you forget your troubles and laugh.

In this book, I'll share with you my ideas on how to improvise successfully and present you some of the great improv warm up games, exercises and forms. We will review how they are played and what improv skills they work on developing. I did not create these improvisations. I did tweak a couple of them. I'm certainly not the be-all, end-all word on how to play them. I'm simply providing a description of them and my ideas for how you should approach performing them. Don't be afraid to question my "take" and try a different approach. Remember that class is for learning, but also for experimenting and taking artistic chances.

In rehearsing the play *Frost/Nixon* Frank Langella was finding it challenging to play Nixon. He told *The Wall Street Journal* that he remembered something he had learned as a young student, which was to allow himself to "be terrible." By permitting himself this leeway, he was able to develop the role with each rehearsal because he freed himself from being concerned about how well he was doing any given day. For this performance, he received the Tony-Award and was nominated for the Oscar when the play became a film. Allow yourself that same artistic freedom; don't be afraid to "be terrible" when you improvise.

Find a class in your area by using the Internet - craigslist.org is a wonderful resource - as well as *Back Stage*, the weekly paper on the performing arts that is also online. If there's no class near you – heck, just use this book with some friends to find your own improv path.

There is a great and mutually-supportive community of performing artists out there. A few people may not be so supportive – and often tend to be louder-voiced when it comes to expressing their opinion. They may not agree with some of the points made here. All I can tell you is what I tell all my students: study with different teachers, read different texts, find out what works for you.

I think you will find a lot that works for you in this book.

QUICK START GUIDE

This book is organized to present to you my improv technique and then lists and describes improvisation warm ups, exercises and games. The terms actor, student, performer and improviser are used synonymously. Pages 7-10 provide an overview of what it takes to get an improv started. Read it now, and after reading the details of the GS IMPROV technique in pages 11-46, be sure to read it again.

WHO-WHAT-WHERE: The job of the improviser is to make it clear to the audience who the characters are to one another, what is going on and where the scene is taking place.

You begin to establish the **WHERE** by starting every improvisation with spacework. Spacework, the pantomiming of activity, comes before dialogue. It does not have to be elaborate, but it does have to be ongoing – you do it before dialogue begins *and continue doing it* throughout the course of the scene. You do not do spacework at the start and then just stand around trading lines of dialogue. That is charmless. We want charm in our improvisations. Acting is doing, so stay active in your improvisations. Also, pantomime all objects, even those you may actually happen to have on your person. By observing this rule, you avoid distracting the audience by presenting a scene that uses a mix of real and imaginary objects.

You establish the **WHO** in the scene by playing characters who know one another. Avoid playing strangers. The characters can have a close relationship, but even a casual connection will suffice. A doorman and the widow living in the apartment building can work as well as the relationship of parent and child. We avoid playing strangers because stage time is precious and we do not want to bore the audience by making them watch two strangers get acquainted. In addition, strangers are limited in how they can interact with one another. In real life, if you behave rudely, or act oddly, a stranger will walk away whereas someone who knows you, like a spouse, does not have the same option. Just ask my wife.

You establish the **WHAT** of the scene by making statements to one another. Avoid asking questions. What is going on must be something very important to the characters in the scene. Also, work from agreement, which means that if the other character wants something from your character give it to them, and then add something about what your character wants. If you fail to work from agreement, you run the risk of the scene getting stalled by a yes-you-will/no-I-won't back and forth between the actors.

Improvisations generally begin with two people onstage.

1. The teacher or audience (whether a paying audience for a show or fellow students in a class) provides an input.

2. The actors consider (silently to themselves) how the input relates to either the WHO, WHAT or WHERE of the scene. Then it's up to each one to round things out by making their choices for the remaining two elements.

3. One of the actors, having made a choice for all three WHO-WHAT-WHERE elements of the scene, begins by tapping the other person on the shoulder and then performing spacework. By starting the work, this actor becomes *the initiator*. The other actor is now *the supporter*, and can forget their ideas about WHO-WHAT-WHERE because they MUST follow the initiator's lead - they *support* the choices of the initiator. (Supporters are not in inferior positions; they simply have to support the start of the scene. After that, both can make choices that establish

the story, and both should support each other's choices.)

4. While initiators do their spacework, supporters don't just stand there. They begin doing their own spacework. Unsure what to do? Often, simply mimicking the initiator works.
5. Eventually the initiator will deliver the first line of dialogue.
6. The students trade lines of dialogue, clearly establishing the WHO-WHAT-WHERE, working from agreement and continuing to do spacework.
7. The improvisation eventually ends. This happens either by the lights being completely dimmed during a show (a blackout), or by the instructor calling 'blackout' during a class.

END OF QUICK START GUIDE

THE GS IMPROV TECHNIQUE

Great improvisations are memorable.

After teaching class one night, I was talking with Kevin. He's been with me since my very first class and is a charter member of the performance troupe I founded, *KLAATU*. Something we had worked on that night reminded us of an improv we'd done in a performance in the same place...some seven years earlier - a scene set at the Battle of Gettysburg involving a Confederate major, a loyal farmhand and the lady who owned the spread and was ever-so-conveniently of the Southern persuasion.

Just as my eleventh year of teaching began, Jason Gordon passed away. He was also a student from my first class who became an original member of the troupe. He moved to San Diego in 2005 and died there suddenly from a heart ailment in February of 2007. I was able to create a tribute page on my website (www.gsimprov.com) quickly because it was very easy to remember so many wonderful improvs he had done over the years, both onstage and in class.

These two examples illustrate how it works. You perform a special improv and it is something you, and others, will remember. I hope you are reading this book so that you can get in the game and make your own memories. Let's get started.

Some people wonder how improv, no less an improv technique, can be learned. After all, it's all made up every time, isn't it? The thing people don't realize is that there are many different improv exercises, games and forms – each with its own set of rules and structure. Where there is structure there is the opportunity for rehearsal, practice and mastery. So, yes, you can learn how to improvise.

But before learning about specific improvisations, you should know that you can develop a sound technique which can be applied to any improv form. The core of the GS IMPROV technique is to always be thinking in terms of who, what and where. These are the pillars upon which you build effective improvisations.

ESTABLISHING WHO THE CHARACTERS ARE

Who are the characters in the scene? What is their relationship to one another?

They should know one another on some level. When you are first starting to improvise, a good place to start is to rely on some basic relationships: parent/child, husband/wife, supervisor/employee, teacher/student, etc.

As you gain experience, challenge yourself to work with different relationships – business partners, political running mates, prisoner and pen-pal, shipwreck survivors or even something as casual as the nodding acquaintance between a regular customer at a bakery and the person behind the counter.

The point here is to avoid being strangers.

Why?

If you start the scene as strangers, you have to spend some of that precious stage time getting to know one another, and usually that is not very interesting for the audience. So start as characters who already know one another.

What do you do when the premise for the scene seems to suggest that it is between strangers, such as a scene about people on a blind-date? Well, you could start the scene during dessert, inferring that the characters have already had their meal, gotten acquainted and have either fallen madly in love or realize it is not quite time to cancel their Match.com account.

A truly awful trick used by improvisers who realize they are playing a scene between strangers is to have someone's character suddenly realize they went to high school with the other person. Try to avoid putting yourself in this position.

As you are making choices of characters that know one another, think also about the aspect of *status*. For example, a parent has the superior status to a child. The work supervisor has superior status to the employee. Consider the implied status in the relationship you have chosen for your improv. In some scenes, an interesting element of the scene is how status changes. In improvisations where the characters start off on an apparently equal footing, the interesting thing can be how the characters compete with one another for the higher status; the upper hand. This is not to say that every scene is about trying to flip status on its head. As you gain experience in improvising you will start to develop a second sense for what is going on in a given scene. "Oh! This is a scene where we are changing status," you will think to yourself, and things will fall into place accordingly.

ESTABLISHING WHERE THE SCENE TAKES PLACE

Scenes happen somewhere. An improvisation is not about two improvisers standing around onstage trading lines of dialogue.

Honestly.

I think some people are scared away from improv because they think they have to be superbly witty creators of dialogue in order to be good at improv. **Not True!** Being good at coming up with dialogue is an asset, but you make your improvisations come alive by starting improvs, not with dialogue, but by doing *spacework*.

Spacework is the pantomiming of a specific action.

For example, before beginning your witty dialogue, you could start the scene by setting your Rolex watch, tying the laces of your brown Bruno Magli shoes, splitting rails in Illinois or building a shelter in Manhattan to protect you from a sudden, devastating climate change due to global warming — just be sure to watch out for the wolves let loose from the zoo, Jake!

Be in the habit of starting your scenes with a minimum of 10-15 seconds of spacework before dialogue begins. Just as important, keep doing spacework throughout the scene! Even if it feels awkward at first, force yourself. The instructor must make sure students do it **every time** they improvise. Why? Because in real life, people do things while talking to other people and you want your improvisations to mimic real life.

USING THE FOURTH WALL EFFECTIVELY

In the theater, when you are facing the audience, the fourth wall is the imaginary separation between the improvisers onstage and the audience. The improviser needs to be always aware of it and strives to stay *open* to the audience, which means facing them to some degree, for as much of the scene as possible. In other words, no more than you would pick up the Irish Spring in a supermax prison shower; *avoid turning your back to the audience.*

Using the imaginary fourth wall effectively can mean that in a scene set in a laundromat, you place the machines "against" the fourth wall. This lets you face the audience as you do your spacework of putting laundry into the washer. If you are in an auto repair shop, maybe you want the front of the car to be on the fourth wall because you are doing work under the hood. Maybe you want it to face the other direction and place the side of the car on the fourth wall because you have to change a flat tire.

Using the fourth wall effectively not only keeps you open to the audience; it also helps you avoid walking through an object (i.e., a buzzsaw) that a scene-partner's spacework established as being in a certain place on the stage.

Keeping track of your spacework is important. Once something such as a desk, car or bed is established as being somewhere onstage, you don't want anybody in the scene to be walking through it. The instructor should make choices that enable the improvisers in the scene to remain visually connected, to see what each one is doing in the scene. When the form permits improvisers to enter a scene, the instructor should position them on the sidelines so that they can see what is being established in the scene. Instead of waiting backstage and out-of-sight, they should be beside the stage or standing upstage. In performance situations, an audience will understand that the improvisers are not yet part of the scene.

Also, when handling an imaginary object, be it a glass, a newspaper or lightsaber; remember that it does not magically appear from thin air. You get it from someplace specific – a cabinet, a tabletop or a gym bag, for example, and you want to get in the habit of using it and then *putting it down*. When you keep handling something imaginary, you run the risk of becoming distracted and losing track of it. All of a sudden the glass you were handling is gone – poof – and then it seems to magically reappear when needed. Audiences notice this and will not excuse it. So use those imaginary items and put them away. An exception: the one time something must magically appear from out of nowhere, for effect, is when you are performing an improvisation and suddenly the scene must continue in the style of **"film noir"** – a genre first popularized in movies of the 1940s. Examples are *The Maltese Falcon* with Humphrey Bogart and *Chinatown* with Jack Nicholson. When an improv scene begins in the style of film noir, you absolutely want a cigarette to magically, immediately appear in the hand of every person onstage. Laughter ensues. Guaranteed.

ESTABLISHING WHAT IS GOING ON

WHAT is going on? After you get things going with your spacework, the dialogue begins. Within the first few lines of dialogue, it must be clear who you are to one another – don't be strangers – and **what the heck**

is going on. (Beginning improvisers should spend a lot of time working on the improv exercise *THREE SENTENCES* page 120.) You develop the scene's storyline, the what-is-going-on by making statements to one another.

Avoid asking questions! Asking questions is a no-no because when you ask a question you are not helping to move the story along. You are taking a pass on doing that and handing the burden off to the other person in the scene. So remember to make statements. The just mentioned THREE SENTENCES exercise really forces the improviser to take a few extra moments before they make a dialogue choice. That exercise teaches you that you have a lot more time onstage than you might think – there is no need to rush. If you find you are in the habit of asking too many questions during a scene, you are probably rushing into your dialogue choices. By relaxing and taking an extra moment before speaking you will find that you can change your question into a statement. Consider how you would like your question to be answered. Then make the answer into your statement. "What do you want for dinner?" becomes "I made fish sticks for dinner." Yummmmm....fish sticks.

So you need to make statements, but just what do you say?

It is important to make the stakes of the scene high. For example, why is today's trip to John's Pizzeria in Yonkers more important than any other? From a conceptual standpoint, scripted work points the way for improvised work. The stories of films and plays are written to tell important truths or convey exciting stories – things happen! So keep the stakes high and make statements that make it clear what those high stakes are about.

Read *Audition* by Michael Shurtleff for more on why it's so important to make "high-stakes" choices when dealing with scripted work. For example, if you read a scene and think your character kind of likes the other character in a scene, you should be auditioning as if you cannot live another moment without them. Think about it. That is simply more interesting than playing it as if you kind of hope they ask you to go out for a soda. Apply this concept of keeping the stakes high to your improvisations.

Consider, for a moment, what makes films interesting. Almost all the classics, even those with lots of action, have at their core the story of a relationship between two key characters. In your improvisations, keep the focus on what is going on between the characters – not what they are doing. When a scene seems to focus on the performance of an activity, I tell the students it's become a "lesson scene" – a scene where we are being shown how to do something. Lesson scenes should be avoided. They are invariably boring. Your spacework *supports* the story going on between the characters, but it does not become the focus of the story; the focus is on what happens between people.

Another important skill in developing the story of what's going on between the characters in your improvisation is to **work from agreement**. When a character in an improvisation wants something from your character, give it to them, but also find something that your character wants. Do not be fooled into thinking that scene is only "interesting" if you deny what the other character wants. You might think that this provides conflict, and conflict will make the scene "interesting." The problem is, though, that if you deny what the other character wants, how does the story move along? You can easily get mired in a yes/no give and take. You want the storyline of your improvisations to move along – for there to be an "arc" to the story: a beginning, middle and end. If you get hung up on keeping what a character wants away from them, then you begin to spiral the storyline – by spiraling I mean that the story gets stuck on one point and, for want of a better metaphor, moves north to south when it should head east to west.

The concept of giving the other character what he or she wants and choosing something your character needs is the concept of "yes, and" – YES I will give you that ride to the airport, AND I would appreciate it if you would repay that $50 I loaned you three months ago to buy *Grand Theft Auto: Vatican City*.

BEING SPECIFIC

Be as specific as you can. If your character is "at work" then you should define what it is that they do; it's a hobby-horse factory, an accounting firm, a jewelry store, etc. It does not really matter what they do because a defined job is always better than undefined. If the scene is set at "home" make it more specific – it's in the kitchen and make that a kitchen in Philadelphia...at night...during a blizzard...in 1956. If your character is drinking a soda, I do not know why saying that it is a

Mr. Pibb is funnier than saying it is a soda, but it is. It just is.

RECAPPING THE THREE W's

So in your improvisations, you want your technique to focus on:
- WHO: Play characters that know one another.
- WHERE: Start with spacework before beginning dialogue and continue spacework throughout the scene.
- WHAT: Make what is going on between the characters important. Make statements to one another. Avoid questions. Be as specific as you can. Work from agreement.

STARTING AN IMPROVISATION

Okay, so there's who-what-where to be considered, and you start with spacework and keep the stakes high while making statements and yeah, you want to be as specific as possible, but – hey! – how do I actually get one of these improv thingies started? Invariably – and in all the improvisations covered in this book – you will be getting some input before the improv begins. This input addresses one of the big three elements of who-what-where. (Furthermore, even though you are being given an input, you often have to make it more specific. For example, if you are given the input of "New York State" you are given the where, but let's make that location more specific – for example, you are on an overlook at Niagara Falls.)

Besides following my thoughts on focusing on who/what/where, here are some technical points, some rules of the road, which combine to form the rest of the GS IMPROV technique.

There are two improvisers onstage. They are standing almost shoulder to shoulder, facing the audience, and are center and upstage. (When facing the audience, to your right is Stage Right, to your left is Stage Left. In front of you is downstage and behind you is upstage.)

Let's say they are given the input of where they are and that input is "the office" – great BBC and NBC television shows, but not the most stimulating input from which to begin an improvisation.

Each improviser silently thinks in terms of the three pillars – who, what, where. In this example, they were given a where: the office, but when it is as generic as that, they should think about making it more specific.

For example, what kind of business is it that the office serves? What city is it in? Is the office on a ground floor or 41 stories up?

Each improviser is making choices that more specifically define "the office." Then they move on to figuring out who the improvisers are to one another – they know one another – maybe they are romantically involved and work together. (You don't have to work for Wal-Mart to know that's a big mistake.)

Then they have to think about what important thing is going on – maybe today is the day one of them decides to start talking about moving in together.

Each person is *quickly* making that who-what-where choice. Like in ten seconds flat. I kid you not. The point is that you don't over think this. Make your choices and let's get the scene going.

Now, telepathy aside, there's no way both improvisers are going to independently come to the same choices. They're also unlikely to both finish making choices for who-what-where at the same time. My preference is that that there's no consulting between the improvisers starting the scene. I don't allow a huddle, because, when I used to, the improvisers seemed unable to quickly come to an agreement. We have to watch, and wait on, their negotiations.

The improviser who first "solves" the three pillars (who-what-where) taps the other person on the shoulder and moves out onstage. The person giving the tap becomes *the initiator*. The tap signals to the other improviser to forget about his or her thoughts on the who/what/where of the scene because now their responsibility is to follow the initiator's lead; we'll call them *the supporter*. The initiator begins moving about the stage doing spacework and will ultimately start the improv with the first line of dialogue.

It's very important to understand the aspect of trust being conveyed in these first moments. The initiator does not have to worry about the supporter saying the scene's first line of dialogue. Both improvisers may comfortably go about doing their spacework because they know that the initiator is the one who delivers that first line of dialogue. **This is one of my unbreakable rules.** The initiator trusts that the supporter will respect this and not speak first. That is important because if the supporter did speak first they might defeat the initiator's intentions for the scene's who-what-where. If the initiator does not get the chance to deliver that first line because the supporter jumps the gun, the instructor stops them, points out the mistake, and restarts the scene.

So, the initiator starts the scene with spacework. The other improviser does spacework too! Do not just stand there watching the first improviser.

Why?

If you do not do spacework it looks like you are an actor wondering what the heck the initiator is doing rather than a character in a scene. Not sure what to do? What does it look like the initiator is doing? If you can make a reasonable guess at that, then you can make a choice for what you're going to do. If you cannot fathom what it is that they are doing, then what to do? Well, mimicking what the other improviser is doing is often a safe choice. Or you could make like you are reading a book, or tying something up with some string. Be sure to make the "something" you are doing specific for yourself. Just don't get so absorbed in what you are doing that you forget that the initiator delivers the first line of dialogue.

Part of the fun, as well as the challenge, of improv is working your way through things that do not quite fit. In this instance, it could be working out something that does not quite seem right with the initial spacework. Let's say you are following the initiator's lead and your spacework is setting your watch. Then the initiator gives the first line of dialogue and makes it clear you are in the age of Julius Caesar. What do you do? What dooooo you do? Well, you don't have to be Karl Malden to conclude that the improviser setting their watch has to *justify*, that is, make sense of, their actions by changing in their head the context of what they were doing. You haven't said anything yet, so even though you know you were "setting a watch," you can still adjust the context for the audience's sake. Perhaps you were fiddling with an amulet strapped to your wrist, or perhaps you were working on a new invention, the wrist sundial. Challenge yourself by doing very specific spacework when following the other person's lead so that you sometimes get into these kinds of "jams." That way you can work on your justifying skills, which are critically important to the successful improviser. The ability to be flexible in your improv thinking will serve you well.

MAKING ALL OBJECTS IMAGINARY

Mime all objects you "use" in an improv. Even if you have the keys, money or candy the scene calls for, just pantomime using the objects. It makes for a much "cleaner" improv if everything is mimed rather than having a mixed bag of actual and imaginary objects. Always using imaginary objects is one of the lessons I learned from John Monteith, who teaches at the great HB Studio in New York City. (In addition to my weekly privately-run classes, since 1997 I have been a substitute teacher at this special, and very affordable, acting institution. Check them out online at www.hbstudio.org.)

Another important rule from Mr. Monteith is that even if things go totally wrong in an improv, you don't sweat it, because "everything is learning for the next time." This concept is really freeing. If you feel like you screwed up an improvisation by making a poor choice or by missing an important point of information – like asking your scene partner out on a date when earlier he called you "sis" – that is not ideal, but relax, it is not a capital offense. You learn from your mistakes, so it is okay to make some! The hope is that, as you get more experience under your belt, you'll be less prone to make those mistakes. As Santayana wrote, "Those who cannot remember the past are condemned to repeat it."

Moreover, do not become the person who judges themselves too harshly; particularly when you are in the midst of doing the improv itself. I have had very talented students in class who were perfectionists to the point that they would not cut themselves a break. After the work is done, yes, you do want to think about what you would like to do differently the next time out, but also give yourself a pat on the back for things done well. More than anything else, let's say you have just done a well-received performance but don't think it was all that great. Then an audience member comes up to you and offers congratulations. **BE GRACIOUS**! Thank them for their support. Don't tell them how you didn't think it was any great shakes. That's another lesson I learned from Mr. Monteith.

I encourage students to perform each improv with the same gusto as if they were doing it for a paying audience. Do that, and also trust your gut. Class is about going with your instinct! See how a choice you make plays out. If it works – great! – good instincts! But it is even better for your development if it does not quite work out. A good teacher helps suggest why things went awry. When the scenario comes up again, whether it is a half hour or years later, you are prepared to deal with it.

There's No I in Improv

In the wonderful book *Truth in Comedy,* one of the tenets is that no "errors" happen onstage. These moments are chances for something wonderful to happen in how the performers adjust and work things out. While I would argue that there are errors committed onstage, I absolutely agree that some of the most charming moments I have seen performed onstage arise from attempts to cover for (justify!) them.

I was once in the audience for a performance at *Chicago City Limits*, a New York City-based group. The scene was about a pair of aspiring-actor roommates who are hanging out at home when the phone rings. Offstage a different improviser is using the theater's soundsystem to "play" the caller. One roommate moves across the room to pick up the phone, and the caller announces, over the sound system, how he is interested in hiring the performer for this great upcoming show they are producing. The other roommate, clear across the room, says "Ask him if there's a part for me."

Now this is either an opportunity or an error, depending on your improv mantra, but it is absolutely something that needs to be worked out. The problem is that the improviser asking his buddy if the producer can find him a part can hear what the caller said because it is coming out for everyone to hear over the sound system. The character he is playing, because he is on the other side of the room, should not be able to hear the caller. What *Truth in Comedy* regards as an opportunity was beautifully realized by the other improviser in the scene. He immediately began smacking at the imaginary phone set and said "This thing is such a piece of garbage! I hate how the speakerphone keeps kicking in."

EMBRACING THE ACTOR/CHARACTER DUALITY

The problem with the improviser hearing the other side of a phone call when he should not be able to demonstrates the issue of the actor/character duality. When you are onstage you are always you, the actor, who is playing a character. Depending on the story being developed in the scene, there are things you may know as the improviser, rather than the character. For example:

- you know that the Titanic sank on its maiden voyage
- or you know the improvisers onstage playing your spouse and best friend are plotting your demise because you, the actor, are standing just offstage and can hear them

- or you know what a show producer is saying to your roommate over the phone because you can hear it over the theater's sound system.

The choice you have to be able to immediately make as the improviser is *what your character should know*. That's the duality.

Clearly the improviser's character should not be able to hear his roommate's phone conversation. If he had not acted like he heard it, then he might have chosen for his character to proceed in the scene by saying how discouraged he was and how good news for someone else was becoming the equivalent of bad news for him. He's using what he, the actor has heard, like everyone else in the theater, about the success coming the way of his fellow improviser's character.

In a scene where the two characters onstage are plotting the offstage character's demise, the improviser might choose to come onstage and make a big deal about how lucky he feels to have the other two as friends. It is also okay for the improviser to come back out and ultimately accuse the other two of plotting his demise, but the challenge for the actor is to avoid making it seem to the audience like they know this because they heard it from just offstage. A corollary to all this is that you cannot stretch too far the audience's acceptance of the conceit that one character standing stage left will not hear the conversation of two characters stage right.

Sometimes, if an improviser is standing so close to a conversing couple that his character must be hearing what they are saying, then they probably should acknowledge it – "I'm standing right here!" or "I can hear you, you know!" and go from there.

The reason you sometimes have to say you can hear what others onstage are saying is because improvisations must always have a ring of truth to them. This applies to slice of life scenes (i.e., struggling-actor roommates) just as much as a sci-fi scene in which improvisers playing the potato and carrot people are fighting the beetle people. The characters have to do things that an audience recognizes as being consistent with how people (or veggie people) behave in real life.

When it comes to dealing with historical improvs, thinking about what you do know and what your character should know becomes critical. A lot of times, you know how the story ends.

I once had the pleasure of taking a class with Anne Jackson, the great actor and teacher, at HB Studio. She told the story of going to see a production of

Our Town and being very impressed with the female lead. She went backstage afterwards to introduce herself and thought maybe she should let the young lady know a little bit about her background. "Oh I know you, Miss Jackson," the girl stopped her, going on to explain that she had held her father in a film (*The Journey*) years ago. The girl was Bryce Dallas Howard and her dad is the actor, now director, Ron Howard. The point of Miss Jackson's story though, was that in doing that performance of *Our Town*, – SPOILER ALERT – Bryce Howard played the role without giving any indication that she knew the character was doomed to an early death. This is something she, as the actress, clearly knew from reading, memorizing, rehearsing and playing the script. She did not fall into the trap of playing the end of the story at the beginning. It might seem obvious that actors should avoid doing this, but they sometimes fail to recognize that it's happening. So, if you get "Titanic" as the basis for your scene, and the scene starts before the iceberg hits, don't let it seem to the audience that your character knows what's going to happen before it does.

ENTERING A SCENE

If an improvisation is clearly taking place within a room – four walls and at least one door – and you decide your character needs permission to enter, make a fist, hold it up and rock it back and forth while saying "knock-knock." Do not stomp on the floor, do not bang your knuckles on the nearest wall (or fellow improviser). That is the convention I like to use. Every teacher has their own peccadilloes about the right way to do a standard task, a "bit of business," onstage. My favorite story is about the teacher who requires his students to 'handle' an imaginary gun, scissors or telephone as if they were dealing with the real thing, rather than resorting to those time-honored ways of holding your fingers to symbolize any of the three examples. (*Time-honored* if you like them; hoary-old-cliché if you don't.) I like doing it the time-honored way because I know the audience will immediately know what the heck I am doing.

I think the point here is that although I was taught in the Air Force "don't sweat the petty stuff; just pet the...well, you know" it really is a good idea for the improviser, and especially those aspiring to perform before an audience, to sweat the petty stuff. Do think about those granular details of what you do when you are onstage and you have to pull a gun, or knock on a door or even how you will introduce and explain an improvisation to an audience.

Knocking for permission to enter is also a great convention because the improvisers already in the room get to say "Who is it?" – one of the very few times you should ask a question in an improv – and then you get to announce who you are by answering "It's your father! Open up!" Good! Now everyone knows who that improviser is playing – someone their characters should recognize on sight. You want to avoid the awkward situation where someone hears a knock at the door, opens it and asks "Who are you?" with the response being "I'm your father."

TAKING FOCUS

In a lot of improvs there are characters that don't start the scene but join it during the course of the action. How you manage that is very important to the continuing flow of the story. When someone enters a scene, the audience's attention goes to them. Embrace the fact that someone joining the scene commands the focus, the spotlight if you will, in that moment. So if you are onstage when someone enters, do not ignore them. More importantly, defer to them.

When you are the one joining the scene you have to take that focus given to you and quickly establish who you are. You should be someone who knows at least one of the characters in the scene. If it seems appropriate for you to walk into the scene without getting permission (knock-knock), then your first line can be a greeting or a declaratory statement using one of the character's names. "Denise, your mother and I were talking and she asked me to bring you this check." Or "Claire, I'm sorry but I'm going to have to arrest you." Remember, remember, remember…avoid playing a stranger.

But besides making it clear who you are when you get there, just what are you bringing to the scene's story to help move it along? What is your character's agenda? Invariably it is determined by the storyline; the "what's-been-going-on" prior to your arrival. Make sure that you are listening to everything that's been established and not wrapped up in what you plan on doing when entering. You can be badly tripped up if you listen to the first bit, make a character/story choice, and fly on in without having heard the last little bit that now makes it impossible for your choice to work.

A helpful bit of advice is to keep the "a small town is a big hell" theory in mind. It means that in a small town everyone knows everyone else's business, which can make for some discomforting situations. The small town/big hell motif can be very helpful for improvisers. If there is a couple arguing while driving their car and someone joins the scene as a motorcycle policeman pulling them over to give a ticket, what are the odds of the officer knowing them? It is much more plausible that the traffic cop knows them if they are all working under the "small town/big hell" conceit. The character of the officer who knows them can then have a lot more significant interaction with them than the mundane writing of a ticket.

Speaking of cars, how do you join a scene in which the two improvisers who started the scene are driving? A nice bit of stage business is to make like you are a tree. Start downstage parallel to the car and then sidestep until you are upstage – you are playing passing scenery. Just be ready if the characters start talking about how they are driving around in circles. It means you've got to keep playing the tree every time they "pass by" again.

Another way to join a car-centered scene was demonstrated by Sean during rehearsal for one of our performances. Pete and Anne were "driving" their car home from a party. Pete was complaining to Anne that her wife character was putting his husband character down during the party. Pete acknowledged that maybe he was no Rhodes' scholar, *and maybe he would mispronounce a word here and there*, but, as his wife, Anne should really cut him some slack.

The scene continues for a bit until Sean enters from the side and sets chairs for the back seat of the car, which he then lies across. Pete and Anne were experienced enough to let Sean do his thing without calling attention to what he was doing; they knew it was the improviser setting up space for the character. In short order, Sean pops up and acts like he's been dozing in the back seat. He then goes on to explain that he's really grateful for them giving him a ride home so he can "see Jennifer Garner on my favorite show, Alias.....or as Pete would call it *'Uh-lie-us'*."

Zing.

Being part of a troupe that works regularly and gets to know one another's rhythm, their onstage "moves," is great fun. When you have had the chance to work together a lot, you can push the envelope and bend the rules a bit. This keeps things fresh by keeping one another on your toes. Or you do it just to bust on one another – for example, when you are driving a car and someone plays a tree, you talk about how you seem to be driving in circles, thus forcing Mr. Tree to have to keep playing it for a while.

People often asked me if the TV show *Who's Line Is It, Anyway?* could possibly be on the up-and-up, insinuating that maybe there was some scripting or heavy editing going on. Besides believing that, yes, it's on the up and up, my sense was that the players had worked together so long, and fielded so many different suggestions, that they knew how to handle anything. They also knew how to keep it fresh for one another by doing things that really depended on the other player being alert. The result is so smooth that it seems like it is scripted. That is where you want to get to: people accuse your improvising of not being improvised.

SEIZING THE SEMINAL MOMENT

What is the significant moment in the scene? The way Sean popped into the car-driving scene with Pete and Anne demonstrates that when you are performing an improv you have to be attuned to picking up on the seminal moment of the scene. The seminal moment is that significant point which you can make the focus of the next part of the scene. In the car scene, the seminal moment was when Pete started talking about how he might not be the brightest guy and *how he'd occasionally mispronounce words*. This is what inspired Sean to work toward his "Alias" joke.

Sean's joke was a great moment. What's important to understand is that the story could continue from that point – the joke did not break the continuity of the scene. In fact, it was a great moment that fed off his character knowing about the husband's sensitivity to being prone to mispronunciations. Keep in mind that the seminal moment is not about what could lead to a good joke; it's the moment that inspires what the focus of the scene can be. Sean built to a funny moment, a joke, but the focus was playing off Pete's character's sensitivity to his shortcomings in this regard.

When we got the suggestion of noisy neighbors for a scene, Lori, one of the two performers starting the scene, made a great choice – her character was painfully soft spoken – the ultimate "low talker." So everyone else in the scene chose to speak at a very high volume. Pretty much everything done in the scene was mundane day-to-day kind of stuff, but we could see the building emotional breakdown of Lori's character, until in the final scene she threatens everyone with a shotgun.

More often than not, the seminal moment arises from something casually said or is a bit of an accidental statement; you mean to say one thing but something different comes out. For example, you've got every intention of saying "a stitch in time saves nine" but it comes out "a stick in time saves nine." During the rest of the scene you might have characters toss off similarly misstated clichés. In this case there is a humorous motif being repeated which is not the focus of the scene, but plays off the character's error. The misspoken cliché may not ultimately be the seminal moment, something more compelling may occur, but it is an important moment which the students embrace, especially because the audience, as is their wont, has likely picked up on it.

A scene about building the Erie Canal might have someone intending to say that they are moving their family to Utica but they accidentally say Utah. So the scene becomes about the family going west. Part of the skill in improv involves selecting the seminal moment and knowing what to seize on and what to let go by.

As you do your scene-oriented improvs you will get a stronger sense of this seminal-moment concept.

BEING FLEXIBLE

Sometimes you will initiate a scene with the best of intentions for making the who/what/where clear. It's clear in your head what your intention is. Still, you may not have articulated it clearly enough for your scene partner. There is also the possibility that you did articulate the idea well but your scene partner missed it.

Perhaps your intention was for the scene to be between a brother and sister, but you do not quite get that across to your scene partner and suddenly they are talking as if you are husband and wife. Guess what? Even though you were the initiator and even if you think you made the relationship clear, you have to let it go and play husband and wife. After all, what's your alternative? Call time and get your scene partner straightened out? No, you keep the flow of the scene going. You never want to "break character" – that is stop playing the character and let the audience "see" you as the improviser. Although I must confess that I do stop playing the character sometimes in performance to comment to the audience. While I wish I could say that doing it comes from having read too much Shakespeare – in which character asides to the audience are common - I think it's due to having watched too many Bob Hope movies. The difference here is that you are in control of the character. You have not lost sense of what is going on in the scene; you have simply made the choice to "freeze" it for the sake of making an aside to the audience. This is mostly about having a sense of showmanship; a feeling for what the audience needs at any given moment. For example, we were well into a performance when we did an improv which led to us doing a takeoff on the film *Titanic*. At one point I said a line that got a groan from the audience. I turned to them and said, as me rather than the character, "Have you been paying no attention to what kind of show this is?" Doing the improvs in this book will help you develop a sense of comic timing which will enable you to know when to give this a try.

The great challenge is when you know, and you know the audience knows, that you have made something clear — we're in Hawaii — and your scene partner acts like it's Cleveland. Try to justify your way out of that one! Do it by coming up with something besides one of you being crazy. Thanks to the television series *LOST,* you might get away with something about your location being mystically relocated.

ONWARD HO

So now that you are armed with an appreciation of the concepts that make up the GS IMPROV technique, it's time to actually start working the exercises, games and forms which will enable you to put them to use. In the descriptions of the improvisations I either use the context of doing them in a class or in an onstage performance. All the improvisations suitable for performance can be used in class, so don't let this confuse you. The most important thing to remember is that everything is learning for the next time. Don't worry about falling on your face the first couple of times out – the important thing is to get out there and start improvising. Acting is doing! Improv is doing!

I sincerely hope that improv brings you the enjoyment it has brought to me.

1. DRAW THE BLANK SPACE

Students take turns drawing on a piece of paper.

Students line up. The instructor tapes a blank piece of paper to the wall and then hands the first student in line a magic marker. That person steps up and draws a line on the paper. Remember, a line can be an arc, a circle, a zigzag or a dot, in addition to being a *straight* line. One-by-one the other students step forward and add their line.

This is a good first exercise for a class because the instructor uses what the students draw to make analogies to improv tenets. For example:

Who builds off what's already been drawn? That's always good. As in improv, you want to take what's already established and work in concert with it.

Who puts a line through what's been drawn, symbolically negating the work? Doing that is not good in the sense that, as in improv, you do not want to indicate that you are ignoring the work other people are doing. The instructor should gently point this out to the student.

Who draws something away from what's been drawn, heading off in a new direction? That is not necessarily a bad thing. If it's early on, you could say that it might be too soon to head off so independently; but if a lot has been drawn, it may be a good time to begin something separate. In improvisations there is that time when the story line has played itself out and so you want to think about moving on to the next, new part of the story. Sometimes a storyline plays out (and the lights do not blackout to end the scene) so someone has to take the story in a new direction.

The instructor reminds the students that in each improvisation the idea is to work together, building off of what's been established, and not to negate it.

"Isn't Hawaii beautiful?"

"What do you mean, 'Hawaii?' We're in Cleveland?"

Let's avoid those exchanges.

This exercise also reminds us that improv is not just a verbal exercise. You should be doing physical things (maybe even something like, yes, drawing lines) rather than trying to fill every moment in an improvisation with dialogue.

2. TOE TOUCH YAAAAAAH

Reach for the sky and emote!

Students stand in a circle. They bend and reach, as best as they can, for their toes. They swing their arms up and extend overhead as they call out a stress-releasing "YAAAAAHHHHHHH."

That's it. Release those stresses of the day, put them out of your mind and now you can enjoy your improv class.

3. ARMS 1-10

Students place their arms in the position called out by instructor.

Another great first exercise for a class, this warm up exercise begins with the students placing their arms at their sides. This is position 0. Don't get your hopes up; this is not leading to ballet.

Having your arms extended overhead is position 10. Holding your arms straight out, perpendicular to the shoulder, is position 5. Working off those three positions, each student figures out for themselves how to position their arms for 1,2,3,4 and 6,7,8,9.

The instructor calls out a number and then students place their arms in the appropriate position.

After a while, the instructor may call out -5, expecting the students to bend their knees and wiggle their arms below the position 0 spot. If the instructor calls out 15, students should get on their tippy-toes and reach for the ceiling.

While it's okay for the instructor to call out numbers other than whole numbers (e.g., 4.5 or 8.25), try to resist the urge to call out "Pi" or "Derek Jeter's uniform number." This is not a trivia contest and you wouldn't want to embarrass a student who's reaching for the ceiling because they don't know that Pi is 3.14 or that the Yankees' captain wears number 2.

A good thing to do is for the instructor to call out a consecutive series of numbers, 2-3-4-5-6 and then 1. After 6 is called, do any students start to move from position 6 to position 7 before realizing that position 1 has been called out? It's not entirely a bad thing in the sense that it shows they have been listening and following where the exercise, and by extension, a scene, is going. However, the point to be also made is that you need to be flexible, to be on your toes for that unexpected turn things might take. "Stay frosty!" as Corporal Hicks advises in *Aliens*. In other words, be cool and stay alert because the next moment in an improv may not be exactly what you anticipated.

4. MIRROR IMAGE

This improv is about trying to move in sync with someone.

Mirror Image is another, and in this case non-verbal, exercise which trains students to stay connected to one another and work as a team.

You need an even number of students in the circle, so the instructor will either participate or step out. Begin with the students alternately calling out "A" and "B." Then have them pair off with, and face, the person next to them so that each pair will have one "A" student and one "B" student.

When the instructor calls "Go," it's the signal for the "A" students to initiate movement. The "B" students must mirror as best as they can what the "A" students are doing. After a while, the instructor calls "Switch!" which means that the "B" students will take the lead. The instructor can switch back and forth as often as desired, but do not switch too rapidly. Give the people leading a while to lead, at least 30 seconds, which might sound short, but is an eternity onstage.

The instructor reminds those leading the movement that the goal is to make it as easy as possible for the other student to follow along. They are not trying to "fake them out" and cause them to fall behind the movement. To facilitate this, those initiating the movement should be going in slow motion.

While you are trying to make it easy for the other student to follow your lead, it is okay and even encouraged, for leaders to move in ways that challenge the students following them. For example, when the leader is facing the other student, swinging their left hand away from the other person, that person should not move their hand toward the leader, because as a mirror image they should also be swinging their hand away.

This exercise will undoubtedly remind improvisers of a certain age of the famous *I Love Lucy* scene with Lucy and Harpo Marx.

5. MOTION CHANGE

This improv challenges a selected student to figure out which of the students in a circle initiates the changing of the motion all are doing.

Students stand in a circle. One student is selected to leave the room. When that person is outside, a student from the circle, or even the instructor, is designated as the person who will be changing the motion.

The students begin to clap, which cues the person outside to return and take their place in the center of the circle. At some point the designated student must change the motion and the others follow their lead. They may go from clapping to finger snapping, or hand waving, or foot stomping, for example.

The person in the center has to make a guess at who's the one changing the motion. If they are right, swell, if not, too bad, but either way, the game ends and the instructor identifies who the designated person was. Someone else goes outside and we start anew. They can wait until a few changes have happened before making their guess, but they cannot wait forever.

The instructor reminds students in the circle to use their peripheral vision so that they do not tip off who the designated motion-changing student is by staring them down.

The person in the center should be rotating slightly every few seconds to lull the designated student into feeling "safe" about changing the motion.

When you are the one guessing, do not let yourself fall into the trap of thinking that the last person you see making the change to the new motion is the one leading the change. You might wonder how someone could think that, but it happens quite often.

The student changing the motion needs to be aggressive also. Try locking eyes with the person in the center and change your motion. I have done this and they still did not guess I was the one changing things. Also, frequent changes make it fun, so don't let a motion go on too long before making a change.

6. PASSING THE CLAP

This warm up has the students in a circle and clapping at one another.

A great exercise for literally warming up, this one gets the blood flowing and, best of all, requires no penicillin.

Students stand in a circle. The instructor makes eye contact with one of the students and claps at them. Student makes eye contact with another person in the circle and claps at them. The process continues for a minute or two. It eventually ends with the instructor "receiving" a clap and not passing it along.

Before starting, the instructor should tell students whether they can or cannot pass the clap right back to the person they just got it from. The latter requires a bit more concentration on the students' part, but also allows the instructor to make a "thinking outside the box" point. The instructor points out to students that it's a perfectly valid option for them to decide, before things get started, who they will send the clap to when someone claps to them. But what if the person they plan to clap to ends up sending them the clap and the rules for this round prohibit them from clapping back to the one who clapped to you? Well, then the student should have pre-chosen a second person they would clap to in case that occurs – their "plan B" if you will. (The instructor should remind everyone that either way – pre-determining or just randomly selecting - is okay.)

The instructor should remind students not to pass the clap until they've made eye contact with the intended recipient. If you have possession of the clap and want to send it along but the person is not looking at you – wait until they do! It might grind things to a halt, but the point of how important eye contact is will be made.

The instructor should point out that students should not be watching the person clapping; they should see who that person is about to clap to. That is the person they should be looking at so they are ready to receive if that person wants to send the clap on along to them.

If two people are standing really close to one another and it's unclear who was being clapped at – even though it should not occur since eye contact is a prerequisite – then one of the two has to "step up" and act with the confidence that they were the one being clapped to, seizing the reins and passing the clap along.

In a variation, students add a word with their clap and build a sentence word by word.

7. SOCK TOSS

Students toss socks to one another in a sequence.

This is another exercise for reinforcing the concept of staying focused and connected with your fellow students.

For this exercise the instructor should have 3-5 rolled up athletic socks – preferably laundered.

Students stand in a circle and raise a hand. The instructor picks a student they will toss to and drops their hand. Then that person points to another person in the circle with a hand still raised, and lowers his or her hand. The process establishes who you are going to toss to and receive from. It continues until one student is left with a hand raised. This person will toss to the instructor, and, as Darth Vader would say, "now the circle is complete."

Remind the students that you are looking for them to make easy, underhand tosses to their designated person in the circle. Nobody should be trying to be the next Nolan Ryan.

Begin by having the students look to the person who pointed at them, causing them to lower their hand –

that's the person who will be tossing the sock to them. They have nothing to do in this improv until they receive the tossed sock from the other person.

The instructor tosses the first sock. Everyone should be looking to the person they are going to be receiving from; don't watch the tossing of the sock, focus on who you're getting it from. As soon as you receive the sock, toss it to the person you selected earlier. As soon as you toss the sock, go back to looking at the person who tossed it to you – you'll understand why in a minute.

Let the first sock get tossed for a couple of cycles to get everyone comfortable with who they are receiving the toss from and then tossing it along to. Then the instructor introduces a second sock into the tossing mix. Now two socks are being tossed about in the same sequence and as things continue the instructor can keep adding socks to the mix.

As more socks get into the mix it is really important for students to maintain focus and remember to return their attention to the person they are receiving from once they make their toss. Once a second sock is introduced, now students also need to stay aware of what is going on elsewhere so they can avoid tossing a sock into another flying sock.

BE CAREFUL! To avoid bumping heads, the instructor should tell students beforehand that when a tossed sock hits the floor they must "FREEZE!" and stand still. The instructor should be the only person who picks a sock up. Let's leave *Safety Last* to Harold Lloyd.

This warm up is great for reinforcing students' ability to focus. It also tries to teach the students collectively to take their time. Do not panic about getting that next toss off and, once more than one sock is flying, stay attuned to what else is going on.

8. COUNTING 1 to 10

Standing in a circle, students try to sequentially call out the numbers from one to ten without two people speaking at the same time.

Students stand in a circle. They will call out the numbers 1-10 in order. Someone says the first number. Anyone is allowed to say the next number. We are talking about whole numbers: 1, 2, 3, 4, 5, 6, 7, 8, 9, and 10. No Pi or 7 & a half allowed. If two or more people speak at the same time, then you have to start all over again.

The instructor should be listening for two or more people speaking at the same time. When/if that happens, the instructor should call out "1" to start things over again.

When the warm up is finished, the instructor should point out that the easiest way to accomplish the goal is for the students to simply go clockwise or counter-clockwise, around the circle, beginning with the person who calls out "1." Just because the instructor said they *could* speak in random order does not mean that they *have* to do that. Admittedly, it is asking something of the students to recognize on the fly that this is a way to go. However, it is an important way of approaching any improvisation. You consider how the improv works and what the best way is to approach it. It's a way of thinking which you want to embrace.

Another important point of the exercise is for students to get involved, not just stand back letting the others do the "heavy lifting" of playing the game. So get involved! You will make Teddy Roosevelt proud. (Roosevelt famously spoke at the Paris Sorbonne about how it is easy, and therefore lamer than Piper Laurie in *The Hustler*, for someone to critique the participant, the man in the arena, when they themselves are not getting into the act.)

9. CIRCLE EXERCISES

Standing in a circle, each student must eventually speak. The multiple variations of the exercise determine what they can say, and when.

The instructor stands with the students in a circle. Everybody turns their head to look at the person on their right. The instructor turns to his left, making eye contact with that person, and says a number to that person – any number at all. Then that person turns to their left and repeats the process, saying a random number. When they're done they should turn back to their right, because the process is going to continue around the circle until the teacher calls "blackout," which is the improv shorthand way of saying "for gosh sake, stop!"

If you want to be Meisner about the exercise, when you are doing it for the first time, everyone should say the same number – and without any inflection! (Google "Meisner Technique" for some background on the acting technique espoused by Sanford Meisner. Better yet, read the book – *Sanford Meisner on Acting* by Sanford Meisner & Dennis Longwell. I find there are many echoes of improv technique in the Meisner philosophy.)

During this variation of the exercise, the instructor should keep an eye out for the wiseguy/gal who calls out "Pi," or "5,234,456" at their turn. The important thing is not what number you say, but that you are focused on making eye contact with the person who says their number to you, and then making eye contact with the person you say your number to.

Once you have the basics down, work your way on to these other variations.

Variation 1: Instead of random numbers, say random words. The instructor uses his judgment on how truly random the words are. Question the students if you think they are being influenced by anything already said. This variation helps teach students to focus. Besides focusing on making eye contact, the student needs to focus on *not* hearing what the other players have said, even though this is contrary to improv basics, where, of course, you do want to be listening.

Variation 2: Hear the word said to you. To the next person you say the first word that pops in your head upon hearing it, and so it goes around the circle. The instructor evaluates if the person is really saying a word inspired by the word just spoken to them, or if they are adding a word which responds to a word spoken three or four steps ago. For example, if the sequence is "cat," "whiskers," "moustache" and the next person says "sandbox" then they're probably reacting to the first word said rather than the last. The instructor should bring this to their attention.

Variation 3: Build a sentence one word at a time. Each word spoken is the next word in a run-on sentence.

Learning the value of conjunctions like "and," "but" and "however" will help you continue sentences which seem to be otherwise finished.

Remember to use adjectives and adverbs. They paint the picture of the sentence.

Encourage students to be positive. There are forms which can make good use of mayhem (bad things happening to the characters) but for this form we want to keep our Pollyanna hats on and stay positive. I think it's a greater challenge to keep positive, happy scenarios going. This variation helps students get into that mindset.

Be specific! So many sentences seem to be about going to "the store." Make the store specific – Target, Sears, Stop & Shop, Gimbels, etc.

The instructor helps the students understand that it's more important to keep the flow going than for the sentence to make sense. This point cannot be overstated. It is very natural to want what is said to make sense and with practice, the sentences will consistently make sense. However, when you are first starting it is absolutely more important for the sentence to just keep going along rather than to worry about it making sense. You do not want the next person in the sentence to hold up the whole thing by turning to the person who just spoke and say "Huh?" "What did you say?" etc. It may well be that the preceding person truly mumbled their word to the point it was unintelligible. Even when that's the case, it is the responsibility of the person who goes next to act like they heard them perfectly clear and keep the sentence advancing. How does the person do this? Make a choice for what you think the word they said is, or should have been. (That preceding person is not allowed to stop things if the choice made is not the word they actually said.)

Keeping things going is a great skill. Sometimes during scenes something goes awry in the storyline. When the scene started it seemed like you and the other person were brother and sister, but now in mid-scene it seems like you're lovers. Putting any weird possibilities aside, would it really help the scene to say "WHOA! Are we siblings or lovers?" Of course not! Keep the scene moving along and let the audience wonder, if they even would, if something seems off.

Variations within this sentence-building format include:

- the sentence has a theme (Hallmark greeting card sentiment, *New York Post* headline, Aphorism, etc) or....

- it is required that the first word begins with a certain letter of the alphabet and each subsequent word has to begin with each subsequent letter of the alphabet; or...

- one person does every other word of the sentence. They start off by facing someone standing in the circle and then moving around the circle (the instructor should not let the person just stand in the center of the circle and slightly turn, they should be almost face-to-face and really have to move around the circle); or...

- the sentence begins and ends with the same person; this puts a burden on the next to last person to "set up" the starting/finishing person so that the sentence can end smoothly. Often the starting/finishing person can wriggle out of a jam by choosing to end the sentence with an adverb (e.g., quickly, sadly, magnificently). Instead of just one trip around the circle, the instructor can specify that they will make "X" number of circuits. If the trips around the circle is 3, then how many words will everyone speak? Well, 3, unless you are the starting/finishing person. They have to say 4 words (X + 1 being the formula for all you Danica McKellar wannabes out there) since they have to start and finish. When playing the improv, a trick to keeping track of the circuits is to keep your hand held at your side and use your fingers to count off.

For example: suppose we're doing one circuit and the sentence built is "Looking everywhere over the very large number seven lot Arthur noticed a big" when it comes back to the beginner. They can add "car" and the sentence makes sense, or at least as much sense as it needs to. But suppose the sentence built is "Looking everywhere over the very large number seven lot Arthur noticed a car" when it comes back to the beginner. That penultimate player did not help set up the finishing person by saying "car" because the sentence seems complete. However you could say "burning" or "moving" or "quickly" (adverb!) to finish and everybody is happy.

- another variation built around limiting the number of words a student can say is that students can add a word to the sentence in random order but must turn around when done. This elimination process results in everyone adding just one word to the sentence. It is almost the same as above, but you do not know who's going to be last when you start. More importantly, players have to get a sense of their being the next-to-last person and attempt to set them up well.

Only the instructor should call '*blackout!*' to end an improv; or '*period!*' to end the sentence-building improv (when required.) Students need to learn early one of the hard facts of improv life. Sometimes you are onstage thinking that the scene has come to the perfect climax and it's time to stand awash in the audience's appreciation, but darned it those stage lights just keep burning on, which means you have to keep the scene plugging along.

Variation 4: This is not a sentence-building exercise. Anybody can start by saying any word they want. The next word said has to begin with the last letter of the word spoken to you. So if someone says "brick," the next word must begin with a "k." A variation within this format is that if the word spoken ends in a vowel, the direction you're going in swings back the other way, and keeps swinging back each time a vowel is spoken.

Homonyms can be tricky. If we're starting and it seems like we'll be going clockwise, and the first person says "know" to the person to their left, then that person should say a word beginning with the letter "W." But maybe they hear that word as "No," or maybe the person to the speaker's right hears it that way. Then the person on the right should/could say a word beginning with "O." Let's further consider that we're in the midst of words going around the circle and someone says "know" or is it "no"? – well if the preceding person's word was "think" then it must be "k-n-o-w" and we continue in the same direction with the next word being one that starts with a "w"; if the preceding person's word was "Klingon," then they are a geek, but more significantly the word spoken after must be "n-o" so we turn back in the opposite direction and it's up to Captain Kirk to come up with a word that begins with "O."

BEWARE! It is possible for a homonym to come up in the midst of play. If someone has to say a word that begins with a "B" and they say "Bye." You don't know just from hearing it whether their intent was "b-y-e" they said or "b-u-y" or "b-y"? Just like Pat and Vanna, we'll call "y" a consonant. So what happens next is up to the people on either side of the person who just spoke; either the preceding person can say something like "enter" or the following person can say "yes." The first to speak defines whether it was "buy" or "bye" – the intent of the person who spoke does not matter.

Finally, it is perfectly legitimate for the speaker to try and fake out the person they are looking at. They may have just said a word that they know ends in a vowel, so they know that play should turn back in the opposite direction, but they keep looking to the next person as if all is okeley-dokeley.

Whatever variation is used, the true point of the exercise, the main skill being developed, is staying in contact, staying connected, with your partner in the moment – the person saying the word to you.

10. RHYMING COUPLETS

Students work in teams of two to come up with a rhyming couplet.

Students stand in a circle.

The first student says a line to the student on their left. The line should end in an easy-to-rhyme-with word. A great choice is a three-letter word. The line should also be about six to eight words long.

The next student repeats the line they were given and adds their own. The last word of the sentence they are adding rhymes with the last word of the sentence they were given. The length of the sentence should be about the same.

As with other rhyming forms where you must quickly choose a rhyming word, like *limericks* and *da-doo-ron-ron*, the trick to this is to select your rhyming word as soon as you hear the last word of the first person's sentence. Then you figure out how to start your sentence so that it moves to that word. It may seem a tricky thing, but it will become second nature with practice.

These first and second lines form the rhyming couplet. Once it is completed, the person who added the second line begins a completely new and separate rhyming couplet by saying a line to the person to their left and the process starts over.

In a slight variation, each line must end with some physical (but not gymnastic) action on the part of the student. The next student repeats the line and the action and then adds their rhyming line and action. This might seem difficult. It is, but remember to take your time when doing it and all will be well.

The reason I write "not gymnastic" is that the idea is that everyone goes home in the same condition in which they arrived. If someone in a class cannot adhere to that rule because they think they've got a God-given right to bounce off the walls, then they have to go. They're risking their health and those of their scene partners.

11. SLAP CLAP SNAP SPEAK

Students have to say a word that fits in a given category after doing some hand gymnastics.

Students stand in a circle.

The instructor gives the students a category. Let's say "Magazine Titles." Then the instructor selects a student who will speak first, and determines the direction the game will move in.

Everyone slaps their thighs, then claps their hands, then snaps their fingers in unison and then the student the teacher selected speaks. The student says the name of a magazine since that is the category. (See how long things go before some dude says *"Playboy."*) Then everyone slaps their thighs, then claps their hands, then snaps their fingers and then the next student speaks, saying a different magazine title.

To familiarize students with the play of the form you can permit them to repeat something already said, but generally speaking, students cannot repeat something already given. I, because I'm just that kind of guy, allow students to say "pass" one time per category.

The game continues with the same category until someone is stumped or repeats something which has already been said. At that juncture the instructor gives the students a new category and the game starts over with the person who was just stumped.

The instructor should encourage students to always have two possible answers in mind. That's because when you think you've got a super-clever response it's the person who goes just before you who says the exact same thing. Then you're really on the spot. Having those two possible responses in mind is your guard against this. When you're listening to what the other students say and you hear one of your two choices spoken, you toss it out and come up with another possible response to take its place. (Of course, then you have to think about whether that new choice is also one that has been said already.)

Even in a simple warmup like this, teamwork skills can be reinforced. Let's say the category is "American Presidents." If you feel pretty well versed in the category but sense that others are not, then you should use your turn to say one of the more obscure responses. You might say "Van Buren" in order to leave "Kennedy" for someone else to say.

When the category is broad, let's say "Food" then a good tact is to narrow the category down for yourself. Maybe you choose to think about vegetables. A corollary to this is that when you're listening to what others say – because you don't want to repeat – also be listening to pick up on other options they might touch upon. In this example, if you're thinking about vegetables and someone names a dessert, this might help you if you're having trouble coming up with the name of another vegetable – switch to desserts. If the category is magazine titles and you've been thinking of fashion magazines and someone says *"Business Week,"* you might begin thinking of other business-related titles.

It's quite common for students to repeat something that was only recently said. I think that happens because they're only half listening to what the others are saying. This allows one of those already-used responses to get in their subconscious and then get blurted out.

The instructor can have some fun with the group by counting how many people there are in the circle, let's say it's eight, and telling them that the category is "Whole Numbers from 1 thru 7." Will they realize that saying the numbers in order might be preferable? Will they remember to say "pass" to protect themselves?

Some categories I've used in class include:

African Nations	Beatles Song Titles
Beverages	Birds
Body Parts	Clothing
Colors	Computer Parts
Currencies	Fictional Detectives
European Cities	Famous Pauls
Flowers	Games You Gamble On
Holidays	Ice Cream Flavors
Liquor	Magazine Titles
Makeup Brands	Modes of Transportation
Pizza Toppings	Shakespearean Plays
Sports Team Names	Steven King Book Titles
Tom Cruise Film Titles	US Presidents.

12. TOSS CHALLENGE

One student competes against the rest in naming items that fit in a given category.

Here's an exercise which pits a person against the rest of the students. Have the students line up shoulder-to-shoulder facing the same direction. Select a student to come out and face the others. Give that person a rolled-up athletic sock. The instructor names a category – let's say it is "Magazine Titles."

The person with the sock is playing against everyone else. They toss the sock to someone and it always comes back to them on the next toss. They start things rolling by naming a magazine and then GENTLY tossing the sock underhand to someone in line. The student who catches the sock must name a different magazine title and then gently toss the sock back. That person says another magazine title and tosses the sock back to someone in line. This process continues until someone cannot name a magazine title, or says one that's already been said.

Before starting, the instructor should point out that the goal for the person facing the other students is to give themselves the best chance of winning. And they win by making one of the students facing them either say a title already said or be unable to say a new one. So the person facing the other students is really on the spot. They have to name every other magazine title said. What can they do to improve their odds?

Try a little reverse-engineering. What is it that puts them at such a disadvantage relative to the others? Right! They have to go every other time. So they should level the playing field by tossing the sock back to the same person each time. Now it's mano-a-mano and they have a 50/50 chance of winning. Nobody said they had to move up and down the line of students facing them. The instructor should not give this away until the exercise is over or until someone's figured it out and does it.

As with the SLAP-CLAP-SNAP-SPEAK exercise, students should be open to "new avenues" introduced by what someone else adds. For example, if the category is magazines and someone answers "*Sports Illustrated*" this might be a reminder to others that sports-themed magazines are a viable sub-category. In a similar vein, if you're given a broad category, say "Shakespearean Characters," try to focus on the play you know best, say it's *King Lear,* and keep in mind those character names as answers.

Moreover, and as with SLAP-CLAP-SNAP-SPEAK, you should have two possible responses in mind. That's because if you only have one, and however clever or obscure you think it might be, if the person immediately preceding you says it, you're toast.

Unlike SLAP-CLAP-SNAP-SPEAK you cannot say "pass" one time per category.

13. LIMERICKS

Students build a limerick line-by-line.

Tough as it is to believe, limericks are not always dirty.

A limerick is a five-line poem, whose rhyme scheme is A-A-B-B-A.

What is an A-A-B-B-A rhyme scheme? It means that the last words of each of the five lines rhyme according to this pattern. The last words of lines 1, 2 and 5 rhyme, as do the last words of sentences 3 and 4 (but they don't rhyme with 1, 2 and 5).

Ideally, you do the exercise with 5 people. One initiates and the others follow from there in order. With fewer than 5, just circle around and double up. VARIATION: With a large circle of people, you can have someone initiate (that is, give the first line) and then people can randomly add the following lines. In this variation, nobody should do more than one of the five lines. Here's an example of a limerick:

There once was a man from New **York.**

Who was an incredible **dork.**

He taught an improv **class.**

Which everyone did **pass.**

Including a plant and a ***stork***.

Let's agree that the lines of the limerick correspond to positions that people are standing in. Five students stand in positions 1 thru 5. Position 1 starts with a line of about 6 to 8 beats (syllables). Position 2 adds a line and the last word must rhyme with line 1's last word. Position 3 adds a line, and must be sure that their last word DOES NOT rhyme with lines 1 and 2. Their line is usually about two beats less than lines 1 and 2. Position 4 then adds a line, the last word rhyming with line 3. Position 5 ends with a line, the last word of which rhymes with the last word of lines 1 and 2.

It's up to the people in positions 1 and 3 to end their lines with easy-to-rhyme-with words. Three-letter words are generally a good bet, whereas "Philadelphia" and "orange" are not.

If you get a word that seems impossible to rhyme with, there are three options: make up a gibberish word that rhymes, simply end your line with the same word or, if that tricky to rhyme with word is multi-syllabic, rhyme with the last syllable. Often, in this case, your line is usually a commentary on how the last person set you up badly, rather than something that builds on the storyline of the limerick.)

The people in positions 2 and 4 are challenged to immediately rhyme with the preceding lines. Though it might seem counter-intuitive at first, you start with the end. Which is to say, when you are in either of those positions, the way to approach it is to hear your predecessor's last word and immediately pick a word that rhymes with it. Then you make your line progress to that ending word. This may seem odd at first, but with practice you will develop a facility for choosing the right word and using it in sentences that make sense in the context of the developing limerick.

When first learning this exercise, the emphasis is more on getting the rhyme scheme down than it is on the limerick being funny, or even, for that matter, making sense. As you develop your skill in this form by practicing, you will develop "funny" limericks because each line will further the story begun by the preceding lines.

Because the limerick exercise is a "stand-alone" form you can be a little more profane, scatological or hammy. It's not a scene where there's give and take; once your predecessors do their thing it's over for them and you won't mess them up. However, you still need to be a team-player in the sense of building the story of the limerick, rather than just blurting out some "wacky" line that has nothing to do with anything already established.

In this form "mayhem" is also a good choice. "Mayhem" means that something physical happens to the central character in your limerick – think of Wyle E. Coyote from the *Roadrunner* cartoons. A mayhem-oriented way to start, for example:

I took my lawyer down to the ***dock,***
And smashed his head with a big ***rock***.

14. DA DOO RON RON

Da-doo-ron-ron is an exercise which is partly an homage to The Crystals early 1960s hit of the same name. It's a singing version of the limerick exercise...but with a chorus and slightly different rhyme scheme.

The rhyme scheme is A-A-B-B-B, with a chorus chiming in after lines 1, 2, and 5.

Ideally, you do the exercise with 5 people, with one initiating the action and then you go around the circle in order. Everyone performs the chorus when its turn comes up.

An example of the A-A-B-B-B rhyme scheme is:

I'm married to a jerk whose name is **Ted**,
  CHORUS: Da-doo-ron-ron, da-doo-ron-ron
He's none to great in our marital **bed**,
  CHORUS: Da-doo-ron-ron, da-doo-ron-ron
Yeah, he thinks he's so darn **sleek**,
Yeah, but he's such a gosh darn **geek**,
Yeah, I think I'll leave him next **week**.
CHORUS: Da-doo-ron-ron, da-doo-ron-ron

So, the last word of line 2 rhymes with the last word of line 1.

The last words of lines 4 & 5 rhyme with line 3.

The students doing lines 1 and 3 should end their lines with easy-to-rhyme-with words. They want to set up the people following them.

The person doing line 3 has to especially remember NOT to rhyme with lines 1 and 2.

If you are doing lines 2 or 4, as soon as you hear the last word of the preceding line, first pick a word that rhymes with it and then have your sentence build towards that word.

Because this is a stand-alone improv – which is to say that you do your improv thing with the focus entirely on you and then you're done – you can be a bit more profane or scatological than you might otherwise be when working on a scene. *Mayhem* is often a good choice - something physical happens to the character being sung about. Repeating our example from the previous exercise:

"I took my boss on down to the dock,"

Da-doo-ron-ron, da-doo-ron-ron

"and hit him there on the head with a rock."

No Christmas bonus for you.

Don't worry about it being funny, or even making great sense as you begin working with this form. The idea is, as always, to get the hang of how the form works first. With practice, your da-doo-ron-rons will improve as you hone your skill doing them.

15. QUESTIONS ONLY

In this two-person exercise the students are only allowed to ask questions of one another.

This exercise runs contrary to the way you should be thinking when improvising. You should be making statements with your improv dialogue rather than asking questions. So this exercise is a good way to help get those questions out of your system and, hopefully, better understand why they pose a problem.

This is also a good exercise to wind down the warm up. Get two students in the center of the circle and let either one start. They have up to a minute. If someone makes a statement rather than asking a question the scene ends before the time is up. If you decide to use this as a warmup-ending exercise, then have the pair sit down once they are done.

The students should still be striving to create a viable who-what-where based scene even though they can only ask questions.

This exercise can help build a skill for "good" question making. Although I constantly critique the students when they ask questions, it's a simple fact that

Greg Sullivan

sometimes a question might be asked during an improv. A "good" question is one which embraces the action that's been going on or helps to move the story along. "Where were you?" isn't as good a choice as "Didn't I see you kissing your ex- last night over by the village fountain?" because the latter is info-packed

16. ENEMY/PROTECTOR

Student tries to keep their protector between them and their enemy.

This form is best suited to young children on a soft, grassy meadow. I sincerely don't recommend using it in class, but if you do, it has to be done in slow motion...literally...very slow motion.

Three students stand as far apart as possible. Each silently selects for themselves one of the others as their enemy and the other as their protector. At the instructor's count of three, they move about in an attempt to keep their protector between them and their enemy.

The point of this exercise is to always be thinking of moving with a purpose. During your less frenetic improvs, the ones in which you are creating a scene, don't just wander about the stage. Movement brings the audience's attention to you, and takes it away from what you, or others in the scene, are saying.

17. PASS THE BUCK

Students stand in a circle. Instructor stands in the center of the circle. This exercise is a contest between those in the circle and the person in the center.

The instructor hands one of the students a dollar bill. (Expect ensuing jokes about pocketing the bill, refunds of tuition and other hilarity.) Students begin to pass the bill around the circle. Their assignment, if you will, is to pass the bill around as quickly as they can.

The person in the center of the circle has their eyes closed. As the bill is being passed around the circle, eventually that person says "STOP!" **and opens their eyes**.

When "Stop!" is heard, the students stop passing the bill around the circle. The student holding the bill begins to say the alphabet in their head.

The person in the center calls out "STOP!" again; it can be said as close to the first saying "STOP!" as the person wants. This second calling out of "STOP!" is the cue for the student holding the dollar bill to call out the letter they are at in the alphabet.

As soon as the letter is called out, the student holding the buck should begin passing the bill around the circle.

The person in the center, upon hearing the letter, should start saying words that begin with that letter. Proper nouns are not allowed.

If the person in the center can say five words that begin with the letter given before the bill can make a circuit around the circle (that is, be passed around the circle until it gets back to the student who began passing it) then the person in the center "wins." If the bill makes a circuit before the person can say the five words then the students in the circle "win." And what have they won, Don Pardo?

The instructor should watch for the student who calls out "X" even though the person in the center said "STOP!" and "STOP!" one atop the other. In fact, "X" should just be booted from the alphabet for this game; it can go off and commiserate with that planet wannabe Pluto.

The instructor should also make sure that the person in the center opens their eyes after saying the first "STOP!" It does make it harder, does add pressure, on the person in the center to have to do their thing while watching the bill make its way around the circle.

A way for the student standing in the center to improve their chances of winning is to think of simple, three-letter words.

The trick to winning for those in the circle is to pass the darn bill faster.

The instructor should base the number of words that have to be said on the size of the circle. Bigger circle…more words.

18. BIPPITTY BIPPITTY BOP

This is another exercise which pits students in a circle against a person standing in the center. Here, the person tries to get one of them to take their place by making them perform one of a series of actions.

The goal of the game is for the person standing in the center to force one of the students in the circle to take their place. This gets accomplished in one of four ways:

    - the person in the center looks at someone and says "Bippitty Bippitty Bop" before they can say "Bop"

    - the person in the center looks at someone and says "Airplane!" and begins counting to 10 as fast as possible. The "Airplane!" cue means that the person being looked at puts forefinger to thumb on each hand, puts them touching one another and raises them to their eyes — they are putting on the pilot goggles; it's very Manfred von Richthofen. The person on either side of Goggles-girl steps to them and thrusts their arm out, forming the wings. (Don't throw a wing into someone else standing in the circle!) If they can get in position before the person in the center counts to ten, all are safe. But if not, then the student out of position becomes the person in the center. When two or more are out of position, the person in the center chooses one.

- another way to get them is for the person in the center to call "Elephant!" The student being looked at bows their head a bit and droops their arm out in front of their face, forming the elephant's trunk. The students on either side of Trunk-man put their outside hand on their hip, each forming an elephantine ear. Then they step towards trunk-man so that all three are hip-to-hip. If they're in place by the count of ten then all are safe.

- the fourth, final and superbly patriotic way of nailing someone in the circle is to call out "1776!" The center person, the one being looked at, acts like they are holding a flagpole – presumably with an imaginary Old Glory flying. The person to their RIGHT acts like they are playing a FLUTE, and the person to their LEFT makes like they are playing a DRUM. Note that the positions and instruments each have the same number of letters – RIGHT=FLUTE, LEFT=DRUM. They've got to the count of ten to get into the right spot.

The person in center must make eye contact with the center-person before calling anything out. No saying "Bippitty, Bippitty" and then making a 180 degree spin for "Bop."

The instructor should monitor that the center person completes "Bippitty, Bippitty, Bop." For some reason, people often fail to say "BOP!" acting as if they are supposed to wait for the other person to say it.

Often the person in the center forgets to call out the 1 thru 10 count when calling Airplane, Elephant or 1776. The instructor should help them out by making the count for them.

What's the point of this exercise? You mean, besides HAVING FUN? Well, it's good practice for the students in the circle to think in terms of relaxing under pressure. There's certainly enough time once they hear "bippitty" to say "bop." Also, they must focus on the things they have to do in case something other than "bippitty-bippitty-bop" is said to them – and the ten count is plenty of time to get into place – if they relax! It's also another classic warm up in which the importance of listening and making eye contact is reinforced; the game doesn't work without it. You have to listen to what the person in the center is saying – don't jump the gun or else you're out. Since the person in the center cannot "sneak up" on someone, the game cannot begin without their making an initial eye contact with someone.

19. MAL OCCHIO

Students look down at the center of a circle. At the count of three they look up at someone else in the circle and hope that person is not looking back at them.

Neither a ballplayer from the '50s nor a "made" man, this exercise helps students get into their seats, making it a great end to the warm up.

We want to encourage students to connect in an improvisation. This fun exercise penalizes them for doing it. Mal Occhio is the Italian term for the "evil eye" and making eye contact in this game is bad news.

Students stand in a circle and look down at the center of the circle.

At the count of three, they look up at someone in the circle. If that person is looking back at them then they both are out and have to sit down.

Repeat until one person is left standing.

You need an odd number of people for this to work, so the instructor has to join in or stay out of the game.

20. GREETING/RESPONSE

A student "greets" another student and receives a reply.

This exercise is another good way to conclude the warm up portion of a class.

Students stand in a circle. A student moves to someone else in the circle and makes a statement, a "greeting," if you will. The other student then makes an ***appropriate*** response. Appropriate is a subjective term. Basically you want the response to match the greeting in tenor and have a sense of being on the same page as where the other student is coming from. For example, if the greeting is "I hate leading us into battle!" the response of "I think I will balance my checkbook now" doesn't quite match.

The first student to provide the greeting stays within the circle. (They will receive the final greeting, which will end the exercise.)

The student who gives the response goes to someone else and gives a greeting and then receives the other student's response. Now that the student has done both ends – receiving a greeting and then making a greeting to someone else, they can take a seat.

Things for the instructor to reinforce:

- Make statements! Don't ask questions. That's the most important thing to learn from the warm up.
- Choose an emotion that goes with your greeting and commit to it.
- Like many warm ups, you will do both sides of the coin - you will initiate dialogue so you can prepare for that moment, but first you must be open to receiving dialogue from someone else.

21. GOING AND TAKING

This is a great exercise for helping students get acquainted with one another's names. It's also a good game for getting re-acquainted after a hiatus.

Students stand in a circle. The instructor announces a destination; let's say it's the beach.

The first student says their name and what they're bringing to the beach. "I'm Pete and I'm bringing SPF 150 Suntan Lotion."

The next student, before stating their name and what they're bringing, must repeat everything that's come before. And so it goes. For example, when you get to student 9, they have to repeat the names and objects of all eight people who went ahead of them before adding their name and object.

As difficult as this might sound, students usually can remember all the names and objects of the people who came before them until they get to the person standing next to them. This happens because they only get to hear that person say their name and object once; everybody else they've heard multiple times. For this reason, before starting the game, the instructor should impress on the students the need to pay special attention to the person who goes just before them.

If someone forgets the object a student was taking, then that student should do a pantomime using the object. If the person still doesn't get it, then just tell them.

The instructor should prompt students with names if they cannot remember.

Ideally, the instructor is last to go so they can show off with the speed with which they knock off everyone's name and object.

A variation on this game is to leave the names out and play in an elimination format. Tell the students a location. The first student says what they are taking there. The next student repeats what the first student says and adds an object. The process continues, with people repeating all the objects being brought, in the order they were added, before adding their own. When someone forgets and object, or skips one, they have to sit down. The game goes on, continuing around the circle, until only one person is standing (but, alas, Jeff Probst isn't there to hand them a check for a million bucks.)

22. WHATCHA DOING

In this exercise, a student in the center of the circle pantomimes an activity they were told to do; when someone asks what they are doing, they tell them to do a different activity.

This form is another good form for concluding the warm up phase of the class because it moves the students from standing in the circle to their seats.

Students stand in a circle. The instructor steps into the middle of the circle and pantomimes something simple; let's say brushing his teeth,

One of the students asks "whatcha doing" and the instructor does not say "brushing my teeth" or, certainly not "Can't you see I'm brushing my teeth!" but instead tells the student a different activity which that person has to step into the center of the circle and start doing after the instructor clears out. The action does not have to be strictly a pantomime. The instructor should use their discretion for whether the students need practice with strictly non-verbal work. When in doubt, make it strictly pantomime.

The instructor should point out to students that this is another of those exercises where the student can prepare one aspect even though they have to be open to receiving something they cannot plan for. When they decide they want to get involved by asking "whatcha doing" they have to be open to whatever they are told to do. Still, they know they will have to eventually tell someone else what to do, and should be planning ahead. Think about what you are going to tell someone to do – that's part of the fun of the exercise. You might tell someone they are "Joan of Arc at the stake," "trying to fit into a small pair of pantyhose" or "baring their soul." Give the person doing the action at least 10-15 seconds before the next person goes in. A nice wrinkle is to use names when asking "Whatcha doing?" as in "Whatcha doing, Sally?"

23. TWO CHAIRS

A student sits in one of two chairs onstage. A second student comes in and follows the first student's lead. Eventually the first student departs. Then a third student comes in and the process begins again.

This is another excellent exercise for ending the warm up portion of the class by moving students from the circle to their chair.

The instructor places two chairs onstage. Usually it's best for the instructor to take a seat first. Being the person already in the seat designates you as the initiator of the scene. One of the students in the circle will take the other seat. You can both be doing spacework but the initiator eventually delivers the first line of dialogue. That's because they have the idea for the who-what-where of the scene.

The scenes should go on for about 60 seconds before the initiator announces they are leaving and explains why. In other words, don't just run away like Good Sir Robin.

The instructor should point out to the students that this is another exercise where they can plan what they'd like to do but must first follow someone else's lead. They can, and should, know what they will do when they are the initiator. First, however, they have to replace someone who's departed and follow the lead of the person already there. They are prepared for the following scene, when they will initiate, by having already made the choice for what they will do. A skill being worked on is the ability to keep that choice in mind after having fully committed to playing the first scene where the other person is initiating.

Students do not have to remain in the seats throughout the entire scene.

The instructor is looking for variety, and specificity, in what the students choose the seats to be. Are they seats in an airplane, a large rock in the wilderness, seats in a theater, dining table seats, thrones, a car, etc?

Many times students think that the initiator must be in one of the two seats. A scene ends and the student slides over to the other seat as if that's the magical initiator chair. The instructor can advise that they don't necessarily have to do that.

24. NUCLEAR CHICKEN

Students stand in a circle to start, but will be moving about shortly, acting as if they are chickens and a nuclear missile is heading their way.

The instructor tells the students that they are chickens in a farmyard. A nuclear missile is unfortunately headed their way and will be striking the area within the minute. (Feel free to substitute meteorite for nuke.) Then tell the students to start acting their chicken role.

After about 30 seconds, stop the students.

Which students went berserk, bouncing off the walls at their impending doom?

That's the wrong choice. What comprehension would a chicken have of a nuke/meteorite? Know your character. Embrace their reality. The "right" choice, if you will, is to act like a chicken just going about his chicken business. That's what makes this an ideal exercise for a first class.

Legend attributes this exercise to Stella Adler. Supposedly there was a student who (correctly) chose to act like a chicken laying an egg when given the exercise. His name was Marlon Brando.

25. MAY I

Students ask for permission to take someone's place in the circle. They receive it!

Knowing one another's names is pretty much a requirement for this one to work. Everyone stands in a circle. One person will ask to take the place of another. The instructor asks a student; let's say her name is Jill, "Jill, may I?"

Jill must immediately respond "Yes, you may."

The instructor, **only upon hearing this permission**, begins to move to Jill's spot in the circle, intending to end up standing where she is.

Once she's given her permission, Jill quickly asks someone else in the circle, let's say it's Mary, "Mary, may I?" and Mary must immediately give her permission, enabling Jill to start moving to Mary's spot, and so it goes.

Instructor must remind students that they cannot move until they get permission.

Once you get permission, take itsy-bitsy baby steps until you see the other person has asked for and received permission to go to a new spot. Once they're moving you can take normal steps and get in their spot.

This form is very good for disciplining the student – you cannot move until you receive permission. It also reminds them that when they are doing a scene they need to work from agreement – the other person wants something (your spot) so give it to them.

26. FREEZE TAG

Students perform a scene until another student "freezes" the action, replaces one of them onstage, and begins a new scene.

This exercise is a good way to end the warm up and is also one of the staples of traditional improv classes. So much a staple that I've all but abandoned it in my class because I think it's gotten to be a bit overused. Still, it does give the students a chance to work on the basics. Those basics being spacework, making sense of a starting position (*justifying* the starting position) and building a strong who-what-where in the first few exchanges of dialogue in the scene. It also helps students develop an "ear" for whether a scene has played itself out because at some point of the scene a student has to "freeze" the action so that the next scene can begin.

Two students start onstage with everyone else upstage. They move about until the instructor calls out "freeze!" which is their cue to stop moving. From this frozen position they begin a scene. It's the responsibility of each person to make sense of what they are doing given the body positioning they are starting from. You don't just move from the position you are "frozen" in to one you think will be more convenient. Make a choice that comes from thinking in terms of what your character may have just been doing or, perhaps, what object they were working with. That decision can help you make a choice for the who-what-where of the scene. Either of the first two people can be the initiator of the scene. After that, it's the person who calls the freeze who begins the subsequent scenes.

At some point in the scene one of the students upstage calls out "Freeze"! The others onstage hold their positions. The student who called freeze comes forward and taps one of the people on the shoulder. They are going to assume that student's position. If you are using freeze tag as an end to the warm ups, then the student tapped can just take a seat. Otherwise they simply return upstage to join the other students, making them also eligible to call the next "Freeze"!

One thing the instructor is especially monitoring in this form is whether the student who called freeze did so at a good moment. It's not a good moment if the scene's just begun and we do not have a clearly defined who-what-where. Nor is it a good moment if the who-what-where's just been established and the scene seems to be picking up steam. Sometimes in their anxiety to get their idea up and running, students jump the gun a bit and prematurely end the current scene. Conversely, you can have a scene that seems like it's been going on forever but nobody is calling a freeze because everyone is stumped for ideas. In cases like these, someone has to be a good soldier and get on out there and get the next scene started. If all else fails, the instructor should call the "Freeze!" and select someone to enter the scene.

Once the exchange of people occurs after the freeze is called, we are in a new scene which has no relation to any preceding scene. The process starts again. It's required that the person who came in to the scene becomes the initiator; they should have an idea for the who-what-where of the scene, which they might have to modify given the opening physical positions.

In a variation of the form, the scenes are related. The instructor can establish that a single story is being told via a series of scenes. This option works best when the students are not leaving the forms and taking seats after being tapped out. This way the character they have chosen to play can return in a subsequent scene.

27. I'M THINKING OF A WORD

This game warms up the grey cells by pitting one student who's selected a word against the rest who are trying to figure out what that word is.

In this warm up exercise a student thinks of a three letter word and the others try and guess what it is by peppering her with questions.

All the students are seated. One stands up in front of the rest and thinks of a three letter word. Let's say that word is "bat." She tells the other students "I'm thinking of a 3-letter word that begins with "B.""

The others begin to pepper her with questions, the answers to which must be three-letter words which begin with "B." The people asking the question are hoping that their answer is the same as the word the person is thinking of. If so, they get to take the person's place and think of a word of their own to challenge the others with.

If someone asks "Do you have wings and fly and sometimes turn into Dracula?" then the standing student says "Yes, the word is bat." They trade places and the game begins anew.

It's generally not that easy.

For one thing, context counts. If the "bat" you are thinking of is the kind you hit a baseball with, then you are allowed to answer "No, I'm not a bat." The students guessing have to remember their homonyms and ask additional questions to eliminate them. For example, "Would Robert DeNiro hit you in the head with this if you let Sean Connery raid your bootlegging operation?"

Usually you get to trade places in another way, by asking a question that stumps her so that she cannot come up with the answer. The game becomes an adventure in which you become something of a New York Times crossword puzzle maker. As you circumverbalize, you try and come up with the word first and then develop some obscurely phrased clues to associate with these simple words. If the word you're thinking of is "cow" then asking "What's brown and white and goes moo?" probably won't be as likely a stumper as "What was the villain in the movie *Top Secret* disguised as when he reveals himself?"

If someone asks "Are you made of tin?" because they think the word is "cog" and the reply is "No, I'm not a can," the game goes on. You don't penalize her for saying "can" because that could be a correct answer to the question. The person asking the question should think of a way to rephrase the question so that the only possible correct answer is "cog."

If the questioner stumps her by asking "What was Barney Miller's job?" and she doesn't know the answer is "cop" because she's an au pair from the Czech Republic and is amazingly doing improv in her second language and has never seen the sitcom, well....tough luck. Since she's been stumped, the questioner gets to take her place.

Before starting, the instructor makes sure everyone knows how many letters the word is. Not defining it makes it too open-ended. However, not defining the number of letters in the word is great if you want to use the game to occupy a room full of kids for, like, ever.

28. CELL PHONE

On a bus, the person sitting next to the window has a cell phone and the person sitting on the aisle needs to borrow it.

Set two chairs next to one another and a third further downstage and stage left. The latter is the bus driver's seat. The first two are the passenger seats. These are the seats that will be occupied. The driver is imaginary.

The instructor should begin by reminding the students that usually you work from agreement. If somebody wants something in a scene, to borrow a cell phone, for example, then working from agreement means that you let them borrow the cell phone (and reveal something your character needs). By negating that in this exercise, we can better understand why it's so important to work from agreement. So, like the Questions Only exercise on page 89, this is a contrarian exercise.

The student stage right, next to the imaginary bus's window, has a cell phone. The person sitting next to them needs to use it. The person needing the cell phone cannot do anything illegal to get the use of the other person's phone.

That's it. Don't give the players any more guidance than that. Just let them go and see what happens. In particular, you want to see how often they choose to start the scene as strangers to one another.

If the students play strangers to one another, it's a mistake. The chief purpose of the exercise is to remind the players how important it is to play characters who know one another. If you are playing strangers to one another, the person who needs to use the phone has little to no leverage. Seeking leverage over the other person is how you attack the game. With leverage you can set up a scenario where the other person is going to look like a complete jerk if they don't loan you that phone.

Parrying the other player's moves is another key aspect of the game. If the person with the cell phone tries "I'd loan you my phone but the battery's dead." You could respond "No problem, I'm a cell phone battery salesman and have a bunch right here."

The borrower is thinking of ways to make the other person look like a jerk. However, a strong offense can be a strong defense, so the person with the phone can also think in terms of making the other one look like a jerk. How? Let's say the person needing the phone establishes they are a doctor and that someone's life depends on their making a call. That puts the person with the phone on the defensive. However, in rebuttal the other person accuses them of being responsible for the death of many patients.

Both students should remember to keep the stakes high, and to do so right from the start.

The person needing the phone says "My god, I know you hate my mother, but if you don't let me call her and remind her to take her medication she'll die!"

Or...

The person with the phone says "I know you want to call your lover, and after just asking me for a divorce!"

The fun of the game is setting these high stakes and seeing if the other person can get their way past that.

Another thing we learn in this simple exercise is the actor/character duality. As the actor you play the character; the actor makes choices for what the character should and should not know. Just because we all know that the person at the window has a cell phone does not mean that they have to acknowledge it. How does the person who needs the phone deal with a character who simply denies they have one? "I can hear it ringing" isn't a bad choice. "I saw you using it five minutes ago." Is another good choice – it reminds us that the best improvs are often ones where we seem to be joining the action in progress. Things happened which we do not see played out.

One of the more interesting starts I saw was by the person who needs the cell phone. They are already on a cell phone – theirs – giving step-by-step instructions for open-heart surgery when their cell phone gives out. How does the person next to the window, the most generous person in the world, the person that the noble doctor is planning on proposing to, deny them the use of their phone for the brief minute it will take to complete the surgery and save that poor young child's life? D'oh!

In class I will do this exercise probably once a year, sometimes varying the setup to make it someone needing to borrow a dollar instead of a cell phone. Even experienced students playing the character needing to borrow the phone will fall into the trap of playing strangers. Reminding students to think in terms of playing characters that know one another is a recurring theme in class.

29. THREE SENTENCES

A student joins another student onstage. They exchange exactly three lines of dialogue. The End.

This exercise helps students build skills to start scenes well by quickly establishing who-what-where. It also reminds the performer to take their time before speaking.

Start with one student onstage. They are the initiator and will deliver the first line of dialogue. They have to start with spacework though.

The scene begins with the start of the spacework as the second student arrives onstage.

The first student says their line of dialogue.

Now is the time for all good men to do nothing! The second person has to resist any urge to immediately respond. Let the line of dialogue spoken by the initiator waft over you. Let it sink in. Let it bounce around in your head for a while. Deconstruct that line of dialogue. Really think through its implications.

Then you can THINK about what your response will be. Do you want to do some spacework before delivering that line? Certainement! So do your spacework and then deliver your line.

The initiator then has to do exactly what the second student just did. Fight the urge to respond immediately. Let the line sink in. Think about what your reply is going to be and then, after having thought it through, say your line.

The pauses between the lines of dialogue ABSOLUTELY should feel uncomfortably odd in their length. If not, then you're not doing the exercise right. The idea is to think before speaking. Even those with a natural facility for always saying the (seemingly) perfect line can benefit. Everyone needs to learn that taking an extra beat allows us to add something even more specific to our response.

The instructor has to make sure the students are exaggerating the time they take before speaking. Put them on a stopwatch if you have to. How much specific information was developed during the three lines? How clearly established was the who-what-where in these three lines of dialogue.

After the third line is spoken, the second student becomes the initiator of the next scene and another student comes in to start the process over. Again, we see an exercise where you know going in to it that you're going to do both sides of the coin. You know that the first time you work you're going to follow an initiator's lead. So all you have to do is be open to what the initiator establishes. You also know that you've got to initiate a scene. So, you can start thinking about what you'll do when you're in that position. It's good to recognize this and be prepared.

30. THREE PART JOKE

Students make up a joke to reinforce the importance of considering the elements of who, what and where.

Three students are onstage. They will assemble a joke a line at a time. The student stage right establishes who and where.

For example, "A chicken walks into a diner."

The student stage center will establish what happens. "The chicken lays an egg."

The student stage left will deliver the punchline. "The chef barbeques the chicken and scrambles the egg."

When done, the student who gave the first line takes a seat, the other two students shift over and the next student comes onstage and takes the stage left position. After each three part joke, a new student rotates in so that everyone eventually gets a chance to perform all three positions.

The instructor points out that this is another of those games where you should be thinking ahead about what you will do when you initiate by giving that first line of who & where. Eventually. Because you have to do the punchline, and then the middle line first.

It's important that the middle line, the "what happens" line, conveys an action. It should never suggest we are about to hear a line of dialogue in the upcoming third part. We don't want to require the punchline to be a line of dialogue. Don't constrain the student doing the third line! For example "A chicken walks into a diner." followed by "The chicken turns to the manager and says..." is not the way you want to play the form. Something *happens* in the second line.

What are the odds of this three line joke being as funny as one carefully crafted over time by a skilled standup comedian? Not very high, but another point of the exercise is that all three players commit to the form and act as if what they are saying is the funniest joke ever told. The true point of the form is to establish who, what and where; being funny is a bonus.

One way to be funny, or funny-ish, is to recognize that this is another stand-alone improvisation. You are not building a scene, so you will not screw up, or show up, your scene partners by being a bit profane, scatological or mayhem-oriented (something bad happens to the character.)

31. YOU DO, I DO

Students sit back to back and talk about their character's actions in a scene.

All too often, scenes become two characters just standing onstage and exchanging lines of dialogue. This exercise helps students think in terms of action. The concept behind the exercise is that the students are really playing a scene. However, instead of them moving around and using dialogue, they remain seated and only talk about what their characters would be doing (NOT saying, but doing). This makes the form another contrarian exercise – we learn what not to do onstage by doing it in an exercise.

Two chairs are placed back to back, but far enough apart so that the students will not knock the back of their heads when sitting down. Students take seats and either one can initiate the exercise.

When the students take their seats they know the gender of the other student and they start thinking about the possible who-what-where of the scene. When they have these elements in mind they can make a choice about what their character would do, given those circumstances.

The students will take turns saying a single sentence which addresses what their character in the scene does; what physical action they take. They do not talk about what their character says, or thinks or begins to suspect, etc. This is about what their character does. Acting is doing. If acting were just about dialogue then "acting" might be called "talking."

The first student says what their character does – "I exit the shower and begin to dry myself with a blue terrycloth towel." (You would not believe how many improvs end up involving someone naked.)

Then the other student speaks. First they must repeat what the other student has said to show that they have been paying attention – "You exit the shower and begin to dry yourself off with a blue terrycloth towel" – do they remember the "blue" or the "terrycloth"? – before they add what their character is doing. "I unlock the red front door and enter the modern living room, returning from my morning jog."

Then it flips back to the other student. They repeat what was just said and then they add their next action. "You enter the modern living room, returning from your morning jog. I go into the bedroom and put on my grey suit."

Keep in mind that the idea here is for the students to be in the same environment, playing a scene as it were, but one without dialogue.

And so it goes until the instructor calls a "blackout" to end the action.

The students are encouraged to keep things simple in their choices for the back and forth of the actions. The point is not to do something "interesting" or "wacky" but to start thinking in terms of how to keep doing things during the course of actual scene work so that it doesn't become just standing around and saying stuff.

The instructor should consider whether the students seem to be on the same page. Do the actions they are talking about seem to "fit" together? For example, if one student is talking about being in a field, saddling a horse and the other talks about taking some carrots to feed to the horse in the barn, then they seem to be too apart from one another to be playing a scene together.

Generally it is best if the timeline for the action is narrow. It is "narrow" if what they talk about doing would happen within a few minutes in real time. It's possible though, for the timeline to be wide. Perhaps someone in our example gets to the point of saying that "You get back under the covers and curl up in bed. I grab my briefcase and lunch and head out the door for the office."

What next?

A possible next choice, made with an eye toward bringing the students back together, "You grab your briefcase and lunch and head out the door for the office. I do my daily tasks and by 6:00pm I am working in the kitchen, putting the final touches on our chicken dinner." This choice intimates that the day has passed and now it's dinner time, which enables the other student to talk about returning from the office.

32. REPAIR SHOP

One by one, students enter and depart an auto repair shop waiting room, adding a random action to an established sequence.

There are two chairs onstage. One student takes a seat. While waiting for a second student to enter they will do something physical (but not too gymnastic). Perhaps they cough.

A second student enters, offers the other student a greeting and takes the other seat. One of the conceits of the exercise is that it's a small town repair shop and in a small town, everyone knows one another (hence, the saying "small town, big hell.")

The student who entered must repeat the first student's action (cough) and then add another action. Perhaps the student rises from their seat and screams "wheee!" Now both students will do the sequence – cough followed by standing and calling "wheee" – in unison, while carrying on a "normal" conversation. They continue to repeat the sequence until the instructor cues the first student to leave by announcing that their car is ready.

A third student enters, offers a greeting and takes the open seat. They will cough, rise from the chair and scream "wheee!" and then add their own action – maybe it's scratching their head.

Now these students carry on their scene, repeating the new sequence of actions, until the instructor calls for a student to exit. It will be the one who has been in the scene the longest. This goes on until all students have entered the scene, repeating the established actions and adding their own.

There are two great challenges here. Continuing, in order, the growing sequence of actions developed while also carrying on a conversation as if oblivious to those physical shenanigans.

This form is a lot of fun and great for lifting the energy in a room.

33. TWO AND ONE

Two students begin a scene and are ultimately joined by a third student, who has been standing just offstage.

This simple form is a great way for students to learn the basic skills of scene-building.

For this exercise I provide the students with the location, but the instructor could give any input you want related to who-what-where.

Even though you are given the where for the scene, ask yourself if it can be made more specific? It should! If you are given "home" – what room is it – dining room, living room, attic? Also, where is home (e.g., Philadelphia, Toronto, Paris). What time of day and what season is it? Make your choice as rich with detail as possible.

I prefer to work it so that men play men and women play women, so part of the starting process involves acknowledging whether it's a male or female student you are working with when you start, and also keeping in mind the gender of the student you know will ultimately be joining the scene. That knowledge helps you settle on the who, your relationship in the scene.

Then you decide on the what – what is going on in the scene – and you make sure that the what is important. For example, let's say that the location given by the instructor is "laundromat." Why is today's visit to the laundromat on Park Avenue in West New York by a husband and wife just shy of their fourth anniversary more important than any previous visit? Is the wife pregnant? Getting a big promotion at work? Being deployed in the military? Or has the husband got something important to reveal? Whatever it is, we want the students to make it important enough to them so that it matters enough for us, the audience, to be drawn into the scene.

Each of the two students starting the scene is considering these three things: who-what-where. When one of them has made a choice for each of these aspects, they tap the other person on the shoulder. This lets that student know that they can forget about the who-what-where they were considering because they are going to follow the lead of the other student. The student who does the tapping is the *initiator* and as such they will start the scene with spacework and will ultimately deliver the first line of dialogue.

I write *ultimately* because the initiator must remember to begin the scene with spacework rather than dialogue. Acting is doing...acting is doing...acting is doing...not just talking. Given the initiator's choice for who-what-where, they should begin with some pantomimed activity that is appropriate to the given location. If that location is a laundromat, then you can be putting clothes in the washer or dryer, or folding the dried clothes or trying to get change from the quarter dispenser (God forbid they ever set the machines up to take those dollar coins the post office machines are always pawning off on us.)

Which begs the question: What does the other student do since all they know at this point is the location that was given? They also need to do spacework – they should not just stand there and watch the other person. The reason you cannot just hang back is because you don't want your scene to look to the audience like one student is already in character doing their thing and the other student is a person waiting to figure out what's going on before they join in. When you're the one following the initiator's lead, which is to say that you are the *supporter* in the scene, take a leap of faith and be active from the beginning. The leap of faith being your confidence in your ability to make sense of your spacework once the other student begins revealing what's going on. Often, your safest bet is to simply do the same thing that the initiator is doing. If you choose to do something different, you can play it safe by keeping it small in scope. That means no big physical action which leaves absolutely no doubt about what you're doing. For example, if you decide your spacework is to change the oil on a car, but the initiator is starting a scene set in the middle ages, you may not be able to pass the spacework off as something else which would make sense in the historical concept. If, however, your spacework is "lacing up your sneakers" you can easily change that to "lacing your leggings."

So, both start with spacework and eventually the initiator delivers the first line of dialogue. Within the first 3-5 exchanges of dialogue the who-what-where of the scene should be clear. If not, then you have a problem. Build the scene by making statements to one another. Avoid asking questions. The initiator should be taking the lead in making the who-what-where clear. If you're following the initiator's lead and after the first couple of lines you know they haven't made things clear, you have just as much right to get involved in doing that as they do.

Sometimes the initiator thinks the relationship is one thing (i.e., husband-wife) but they don't do a good job articulating it. If the other student thinks they are supposed to be brother-sister and starts acting like that's the deal, then what? The initiator has to be flexible and go with the new brother-sister relationship even if that means they cannot proceed with their choice for what's going on. There are no timeouts in improv. It's essential to just keep plugging along, adapting to what the story's become. For example, continuing to talk about making a baby because you want to stay committed to your initial choice of husband-wife as the relationship isn't such a good idea once the characters become brother-sister.

The student offstage will eventually be joining the scene. Generally speaking they should give the two other students about 30 seconds to clearly establish the who-what-where before entering. There are rare exceptions to this rule of thumb. There may be a time when it's helpful for the third student to enter earlier. This is something that you develop an "ear" for through practice. I call it "developing an ear for" because listening is a key for the offstage student. They have the huge actor/character duality advantage. As the actor they are listening to what the other two actors are establishing in the scene. This enables them to make an informed choice of what character they are going to play, what that character should or should not know about what the actors onstage have established, and how their character's appearance is going to help move the story along.

A great way to play TWO AND ONE is to have a scene done as an intentionally dramatic scene and then have the students replay it, following the same storyline and using as much of the same dialogue as possible, but now the scene is being played as intentionally comic. Often, students do not choose to do a dramatic scene. Here's an opportunity to force the issue.

34. EVERY SECOND COUNTS

Two teams of paired students build a scene.

Four students take the stage, pairing off into two teams. Ideally the genders will match up but it's okay if they don't.

Team A is stage right. Team B is stage left.

The input given is a location. The instructor has to keep track of the time.

Team A goes first. One of the two students signals the other via the shoulder tap that they will initiate. They begin with spacework. The clock begins ticking when they speak the first line of dialogue. Team A gets 10 seconds, after which the instructor calls blackout.

Now it is team B's turn. They have to repeat team A's first 10 seconds and then add 10 of their own. Then the action switches back to team A. They repeat the 20 seconds established and add 10 of their own. This process continues until team B completes a 60-second scene.

Part of the challenge is to faithfully recreate what has already been established. While you don't change anything significant to the storyline, it is permissible and even encouraged to "clean up" things. Cleaning up means making changes when you need to clarify things like the relationship, what's going on, or maybe even the location, even though that was given as the input. Sometimes the location can be broad – like "home" – and so you should clarify if you are in the kitchen, or basement, etc.

Once all the students have had a shot at 10-20-30-40-50-60, it's time to follow up with 30-60-90-120. This version of the game gives teams get longer stretches of time to build their scenes and makes the re-creation more challenging.

Both exercises are geared to reinforcing the importance of establishing a specific who-what-where at the start of a scene. The exercise also commands listening on every student's part as they keep track of what the other team establishes. It also helps them develop a sense of time onstage; how long 10 seconds "feels." Students will find they have more time than they think, so they should be able to avoid feeling rushed during their improvisations.

35. WHAT'S GOING ON?

The instructor writes a scenario on a slip of paper and places it onstage. A student steps forward and reads the scenario, then gets two minutes to act it out in pantomime (which means no dialogue or sounds, for those of you who are Marcel Marceau-deficient).

The scenario should be a specific action with two to three additional specifics that can revolve around who-what-where.

For example:

"You are blowing out the candles on your 100th birthday cake on a Christmas morning in Dallas, Texas."

When the first student finishes their two minute pantomime, the instructor asks the other students what's going on. Usually, during the first rounds, I would tell them if they've guessed some elements right, but not tell them which ones. I want them to figure out what's right by comparing what happened in the first scene to what happens in the subsequent scenes. The idea being that the people playing the subsequent scenes would repeat the things which are "correct" in the guesses.

A second student comes up, reads the same scenario, and does two minutes, followed by more discussion before the next student comes up.

The first couple of scenes pretty much set a baseline and should cover all the elements. Subsequent work helps flesh out some of the specific parts.

Of course, every time someone comes up to do a scene you have one less person to guess. After half the class has gone, if the phrase has not been guessed, the instructor tells the students what it was and then they discuss the work and possible other choices. Then try another scenario with the pantomimes done by the people who did not work during the first one.

This exercise is to remind us to keep doing spacework and not depend on dialogue. It doesn't really matter if the phrase is guessed. What matters are the choices made in trying to suggest the phrase to the other students.

Create your own scenarios by thinking in terms of a who-what-where for the lone student onstage. Make every aspect as specific as you can.

36. MYSTERY GUEST

Someone is sent out of the room and is assigned a celebrity of their gender during their absence. When they come back in, it's as if they are fielding questions from a press corps. When they think they know who they are they work an acknowledgment into their dialogue.

Start with a chair center-stage and send one of the students out of the room. They know you will be assigning them the name of a well-known person, living or deceased, real or fictional, who is their gender. When they return, they take the seat and the other students start to pepper them with questions.

Even though the student doesn't know who they've been assigned, they must act like they do from the very first moment. This is the key skill being developed in this improv.

How do they pull that off? If they were actually the character they would know the answer if they were tossed a question like "Are you married?" or "Where do you live?" but since they are not they have to demur if given this kind of question right off the top. So think of the questioning like a presidential debate — answer without answering. "I'd rather not talk about that." Or "I answered that question so many times, can't we have something fresh?"

The role of the questioners is to ask questions with the intent of providing a clue, not to try and stump the student. Your role is actually to help them get it. The challenge for those posing the questions is to ask something that gives a clue without giving it away. So the game play is not just the burden of the student trying to figure out who they've been assigned, but also depends on the skill shown by those asking the questions.

Often, the first few questions may be posed more to elicit a response from the other questioners than to help the "celebrity" student figure out who they've been assigned. They have clever references in them which the other students "get" because they know the name that's been assigned.

For example, if a male student was assigned Sherlock Holmes and the first question is "I'm having a terrible time preparing my taxes, can you help me make some deductions?" The point of the question was to use the word "deductions," because Holmes was renowned for his deductive reasoning. This will probably resonate more with the other students than the person trying to figure out who they are ("hmm, who's a famous IRS agent?" they're thinking) but that's okay.

The first few questions should be geared toward NOT giving it away. The first question to our prospective Mr. Holmes should not be "When you were solving all those mysteries with Doctor Watson in Victorian London, did you ever worry that Moriarty would kill you?" Kind of gives away too much. However, it's a legitimate question to ask if there have already been 20 questions and the student still looks to be totally confused. At that point you want the question to be geared toward basically telling the person who they are.

Sometimes there are people who are so iconic that the most innocent of questions gives things away. Once someone in my class was assigned Marilyn Monroe, and the first question was along the lines of "Today's my birthday, would you mind singing to me?" and the woman immediately knew she was Monroe.

As the student guessing, you should keep in mind that the people asking the questions sometimes screw up, so don't put too much weight behind the clue from any single question. It's the confluence of clues from many questions that helps that light bulb go off over your head. Eureka! I've got it.

Once you think you know who you are, you don't stop the game and turn to the instructor and ask if you're so-and-so. Rather, you work it into the responses you are giving to the questions being asked. "Well, you know, as Sherlock Holmes I was only scared once, when someone stole my Persian slipper after I'd just filled it from a buy." If you are Sherlock, then great, the game is over. But if you were assigned a different person, then the real fun and a great challenge of the game arrives as you have to dig yourself out of the hole your wrong guess has put you in. The audience can help by making some negative sounds – not quite Bronx Cheers thank you – when they sense you are claiming to be someone you are not. "Well, you know, as Sherlock Holmes (naaaa-haaa sounds from audience) I...uh, well...I would be on the case, but I'm not Sherlock Holmes, so, next question."

You can help the person guessing out by:

- asking them how they are enjoying their time in America. Thus indicating that they are foreign.

- prefacing your question with "when you were alive" to let them know that they are not a fictional character and, also, no longer among the living.

- by asking them about "their creator," and not in the intelligent-design vein, it means that you are cluing them in that they are a fictional character.

The instructor watches for three key things:
- Does the student start speaking to who they think they are as soon as they have a sense or do they hold off for more questions, more assurance, before taking that leap of faith?
- Are the questions well conceived or do they give away too much information at the start? If things are dragging then feel free to prompt more obvious-clue questions.
- How well does the student maintain the façade of being the celebrity they've been assigned? Do we see the student sweating it out?

Remind students that the goal is not so much to guess the celebrity assignment but to play the game well. The student guessing has to work on their "veneer of confidence" – carrying themselves at all times as if they actually knew who they were assigned from the get-go.

37. JOB INTERVIEW

A student is assigned a profession while out of the room. They return and are "interviewed" by another student for three minutes, by which time they have to make their guess about what the profession is.

The conceit here is that this is a follow-up, or second, interview, which the student is coming in for. This enables the characters to know one another. Also, the set up could again play off the concept of small town where everyone knows one another, or it could be a friend who's arranged for the job interview at the company where they are already working.

This is a very challenging form in a number of ways.

First, the student trying to guess the job they're interviewing for cannot let it seem that they don't know what the job is. The character they are playing certainly knows the job they are interviewing for. In the same vein, the interviewer cannot say the job, so they are likewise challenged to make the dialogue believable given that constraint.

Usually the interview takes place in an office, but the interviewer can make the location wherever they want. For example, if the job being interviewed for is "gladiator" then it might be helpful for the interview to take place on the floor of Rome's Coliseum. Think about the spacework the interviewer might use before beginning the dialogue.

The challenge to the interviewer is to try and give the other student clues subtly at first and then more directly. If the jobs seem less than run of the mill, it helps the interviewer to think in terms of who it is who would be paying someone to do this.

Some possible jobs to be interviewed for:

Beekeeper	Counterfeiter
French Teacher	Gigolo
Glee Club Tutor	Health Club Sales Staff
Mob Informant	Movie Director
Playboy Photographer	Shaman
TV Weatherman	Vampire Slayer

38. CLICHÉ

The students are split into groups and each group is assigned a familiar phrase. Their task is to act out a story inspired by the phrase. Afterwards the other students are asked to guess what the phrase was.

The instructor splits the students into teams and hands each team a slip of paper with a familiar phrase on it (e.g., "A stitch in time saves nine."- what the heck does that mean, anyhow? - "A rolling stone gathers no moss." etc). The teams are given about five minutes to plot out how they would present a scene inspired by the phrase. For example, there could be a very industrious group of people collecting growth from the north side of trees who are offended that their pal, Keith (Richards) is not helping them out. Mick Jagger's probably more fun to play but could be a straight giveaway. And maybe the moss that's trying to be gathered is the lovely Kate Moss. Or play a scene where the industrious workers are actually walking-talking magazines, and it's Jann Wenner's publication (*Rolling Stone*) that's not holding up its end of the bargain.

Ideally, the scene played stumps the audience as to what the phrase was, but once they are told, everyone says "Of course!" This does not happen all that often, and it's not the goal, per se, because the playing of the scene is what really matters. Do the students, in playing out their vision of the phrase, still try to make the who-what-where of the story clear?

Maybe you have 2, 3 or 4 groups that are going to go. While one is performing, some or all of the groups yet to go may be inclined to try and discuss what they're planning to do, to refine it a bit. This should not be allowed, because their conversation distracts us from the work going on onstage. The instructor must prohibit this.

Variation 1: Just before the first group starts, the instructor announces that the scene is to be played in a certain style (e.g., western, sci-fi, film noir, biblical epic). To be fair, it's probably best to alert all groups before they start their planning that this is coming, but it's good not to tell them what style they are getting until they are just about to go. Messes with their minds! Seriously, it's about training the students to be flexible in working in changes, even when they come from the external (here, the instructor) rather than organically (from what is going on during the course of the scene).

Variation 2: Group scenes are great for building scene-sharing skills. When you end up with more than two people onstage, you have to learn how to "take turns" with dialogue, so that you're all not competing to speak at once. You have to get a sense for who the main characters are and who the supporting players are. So for a variation, instead of group scenes you can play two-person scenes. The two-person scenes make for quicker action and help insure that everyone gets equally involved.

39. 1 to 5 to 1

A student begins with a monologue and is joined by four other students, one at a time, to play new scenes. Then students depart in the order they arrived and we revisit and resolve the scenes previously created. In essence, think of it as climbing a ladder of scenes and then descending that ladder.

There are five students onstage to start and one should be assigned the task of coming forward and beginning a monologue. They are standing in a line, roughly shoulder-to-shoulder, and facing the audience. The student doing the monologue steps forward and asks those seated (or the instructor) for their input: "something that begins with the letter A." (Use whatever letter you like, even "X" especially if you're dying to play five scenes about xylophones.) You can experiment by asking for objects or emotions. You can narrow what you might get further by asking for something you might find in a drugstore, or a garage, etc.

The first student starts the monologue which at some point uses the suggestion. It does not have to be the focal point of the monologue; it just has to be mentioned during the course of the story told. The student should be encouraged to use purposeful movement in telling the monologue. Purposeful movement, as opposed to simply wandering around the stage, enhances the storytelling by acting out some of the physical actions being described.

The other four students will each use the suggestion to start a scene. The challenge is to use it in a different way.

At some point of the monologue, the next student who wants to use the suggestion does a run-around. The run-around involves running from their spot in the back down one side of the stage and across the front. This signals to one and all that what's just been going on is now over and they will be initiating the next new scene. Now the second student begins a scene with the student who was doing the monologue.

It is very important to remember that whenever someone is starting a scene it is their responsibility, and theirs alone, to make the reference to the input. There are two reasons for this: you don't want to have more than one person using up ideas referencing the suggestion during any one scene – leave something for the following students. Also, as in any scene, if you are not the initiator your only job is to follow the initiator's lead. If you start worrying about whether the suggestion has been used and decide to toss in one of your own, you run the risk of finding out later that maybe the initiator did a very subtle reference to the suggestion that went over your head. Finally, in performance you would not want an audience wondering why there are multiple references being made. They might think this is a requirement for the scene when it is not.

Eventually a third student does the run-around and we have a three-player scene with that person and the people who were doing the two-person scene. Then a fourth begins a four-player scene and finally we have the fifth player join and create the five-player scene. Whenever someone does that run-around the students already onstage performing their scene go into a freeze, waiting for the arriving student to start their spacework and ultimately give the first line of this new scene.

Remember, it's the people who join the scene who initiate and have the idea for the who-what-where of each scene.

When the five-player scene starts to feel to the students playing it like it is reaching its conclusion, the person who initiated the scene departs. They don't just wander off the stage! Your character has a reason for going. Say what it is and depart. As we work our way down from the five-person scene back to the monologue, there's no run-around. Students simply depart. So there's no "freeze" cue, per se. It is in the moment that the departing character leaves the stage that we return to the story of the four-person scene, and so on.

Whereas the fourth person to enter had the job for initiating the story of the four-person scene, it's okay for anybody to begin its resolution. It is not required for the resolution to be started by the person who began the scene on the way up. What is important, though, is to avoid having the resolution pick up from the moment where you left off. Invariably this is not the best choice. It's almost always better for the scene to be picked up at a later point in time – it's up to the improviser to determine if that next best moment is an hour later, or a day, year or generation later. Why? It gives you more options. One of those options being the twist-ending popularized so well by *The Twilight Zone*; the conclusion is unexpected, it's a surprise. For example, perhaps an initial three-person scene is between a young woman preparing for her prom who is being raised by her two uncles. In the resolution scene, the young woman may now be in her forties and she's trying to care for her now forgetful uncles. Often, an interesting resolution involves things being turned on their head from the initial scene. The dude who was happy he was going to inherit grandma's money is now sad that she's gone.

The process of revisiting the early scenes continues. The four-person scene is revisited. The person who initially started it will be the person to leave. Then we revisit the three-person scene and eventually its creator leaves. Then the two-person scene is revisited, the student who started it leaves and we are back to the lone student onstage, who will bring their opening monologue to a conclusion.

Again, the student who initiated the scene on the way in does not have to begin its resolution as we revisit the scene. However, that person is required to be the one to leave so that the next scene can be revisited with the same characters we saw in the initial scene. This often gets screwed up as people are getting the hang of the form. You see a lot of students scrambling to prevent someone from departing the stage because they know that person needs to stay.

In forms where a suggestion has to be referred to during the improvisation, it is important to keep in mind that what always matters most is what's going on between the characters in the scene. A clever reference to the suggestion is not going to save a scene where the who-what-where is unclear. That's surrendering the scene to the game, which is putting the achievement of the game's requirement ahead of the making of a good scene. Don't surrender the scene to the game! It's a "Remember the Alamo!" mantra for improvisers.

We used to do this form in our shows but I sensed that it was hard for the audience to get a handle on what was going on. And the form can take a long time, easily 10-15 minutes with five players involved. So it can be a real show-stopper, but not in the good-way, when it's not clicking. It is however, an excellent training form for class and I use it each semester.

40. THE HAROLD

Using a single suggestion, students create a series of scenes which ultimately interconnect.

The legendary improv instructor Del Close (who played the alderman attempting to bribe Elliot Ness in the film *The Untouchables*) is credited with originating this form. Why it was named the Harold has never been clear. It just is.

The Harold is the lynchpin of long-form improvisation. Two great books for learning about long-form improv are *Truth in Comedy*, by Charna Halpern, Del Close and Kim Johnson, and *The Art of Chicago Improv*, by Rob Kozlowski.

Students begin onstage and ask the audience for a suggestion. It could be plain old anything, or can be defined by the troupe – an object that begins with the letter "R," a problem people face, a location. In class I usually give the students the name of an object; in performance we ask for a problem.

Moving stage right to left, each student steps forward and says something inspired by that suggestion: maybe it is making a sound, saying a word, a sentence or a short paragraph which was inspired by the suggestion.

After the last student speaks we go back to the first student and keep on repeating the process.

The things the students are saying are potential scene-starting ideas.

After everyone's had at least one chance to say something they associate with the suggestion, one of the students will step forward. This person has decided how to use one of the suggestions as the basis for starting a scene. They don't have to use one of the ideas they said. They are at liberty to use someone else's idea.

They will be the initiator of the scene and have to select at least one of the other students to begin the scene with. The other students maintain their position, the conceit being that they are transparent to the action of the scene.

Once the scene has started the remaining students have two options. When they are ready to act, they can join the current scene or they can start the next scene. If they choose to join the current scene, the regular rules apply. They should enter appropriately, make it clear who their character is from the start and have a clear idea in their head about what they are bringing to the scene to help move the story along.

If they are starting the next scene, they will use one of the other ideas inspired by the initial suggestion. To begin the next scene, they need to signal the students in the current scene by doing a run-around. They move from where they are standing down one side of the stage and across the front of the stage. A gentle trot is sufficient.

Their run-around signals to those playing the scene that this scene is now over and the next scene is about to start. When they begin that next scene, they have to be the initiator since they have the idea for what come next, and they should also pick at least one other student to start the scene with and be their supporter. The other students should go back to their original positions.

This process continues. Additional scenes are started. Each scene is unique and, at least initially, has no connection to the scenes we saw earlier. In each scene students should play characters that are different from those they established in prior scenes. When first getting students acclimated to the Harold, I suggest you just keep creating new, unique scenes until the use of the initial suggestion seems to have petered out.

With experience, you will want to embrace the challenge of the form. After about five initial scenes, the next scene should "re-visit" an earlier scene with the intent of continuing that scene's story. The already established characters return, but there's also the suggestion that there's a connection to elements of the story from one of the other initial scenes. The reference can be subtle, or can be as blatant as one of the characters from the other story being part of this scene.

Additional scenes are played which also revisit earlier played scenes, each suggesting connections with other scenes, until ultimately there's a final scene in which the storylines culminate and there's a resolution. One or more of the initial scene's storylines may be dropped because the students do not see them as being a good fit.

Think of the Harold as a pyramid of scenes. About five scenes constitute the first level. Then we have levels with four, three and two scenes. Finally there is one scene. Each level further intertwines the storylines. It requires a lot of work and dedication to the form to make it work well.

Some groups employ the Harold in a very specific motif. Perhaps they strive to do a Shakespearean take on the Harold. Some do strictly tragic improv. One wonderful New York City-based group did a musical theater Harold. The first half of their show would present five improvised "Tony-nominated" musical numbers. In the second half of the show you saw the musical from which the winner, as selected by the audience, came.

41. HUMAN ORCHESTRA

Students in a line become their assigned objects and emotions, performing as if they were an orchestra being conducted.

This form is a great performance piece, and one which is especially good to start the show with in order to introduce the entire cast. It's also a great classroom form as it builds some of the great "stand-alone" decision-making skills and truly forces the student to commit to what they've been assigned.

Seven or so students stand in a line facing the rest of the class. An odd number works best as it places someone in the center. For purposes of this description, we'll say the number is seven. The instructor is referred to here as the conductor, because they will cue the action. The students who are watching are the audience and will provide the suggestions. Sometimes the instructor may wish to prepare all the suggestions for objects and emotions in advance so that there's diversity or because they don't "trust" their students not to make only ribald choices. I learned this lesson the hard way and lo the many times I've had to hear the rant of the "Angry Vibrator" in class.

One at a time, moving stage right to left, students will step forward. The instructor, who will become the conductor shortly, asks for objects and assigns them to the students. The students should then repeat the name of their object aloud. This is a good performance habit to get into. Sometimes in shows, you get a suggestion from the audience and it's said loud enough for you to hear it but perhaps not the rest of the audience. So you repeat it aloud to make sure everyone knows what it is.

Once you've repeated your assignment out loud, keep saying it to yourself. Forgetting what you've been given is death to the flow of this form and to any form where the audience has provided you with an assignment.

Then the instructor/conductor goes back to the start of the line and asks for "emotions." As these are called out, the conductor points to the student receiving the assignment. Now here's an exception to the rule of repeating back to the audience the suggestion they give you - rather than repeating the suggested emotion aloud, they should nod back to the instructor to acknowledge that they've heard it. Now they start repeating the assigned emotion-object silently to themselves. Often in performance, instead of just asking for emotions, you may ask for "emotions or states of being." We explain that a "state of being" opens the door for suggestions like "French," "Republican" or "Alien" rather than just emotions.

Now the instructor explains to an imaginary "audience" that she, or he, is the conductor of this human orchestra and that it's time for the orchestra members to remind the audience of their assignments.

One at a time, again moving from stage right to left, students step forward and say their assignments aloud. This is very important: the student is the emotion-object. They are not suggesting that they are simply going to talk about the emotion-object but that they are truly that item in that state, so everyone begins by saying "I'm a" or "I'm an."

"I'm an angry comb!" Display your emotion when making this statement. Pantomime something that suggests your being the object. Get your inner James Brown out and say it, and be it - loud and proud.

Once everyone has reminded the audience of their assignments, the conductor cues them to "warm up their voices." Everyone should start saying "mi-mi-mi" as if they are divas warming up their voices. You don't attempt any specific dialogue. SAVE THE FUNNY

STUFF for when it counts! (In class I shorthand this to "Save the funny.") When it counts is when the spotlight's on you and the spotlight's on you when the conductor cues you to speak by pointing at you.

If you haven't yet, you should begin to appreciate that there's a lot of structure to this form. Structure helps the form flow and, especially in performance, helps to keep the audience in tune with what you are doing. In this specific improv it also helps the students anticipate when their turn is coming up so they can be ready to deliver.

Once everyone in the line has warmed up their voices, the conductor begins the initial pass. The conductor begins with the student stage right and eventually moves along the line until getting to stage left.

When the conductor points at someone it's their cue to begin their dialogue – their rant – as if they actually were their assigned emotion-object. When the conductor points to someone else you stop talking – immediately – and the next person begins.

What do you say? Well, the point of the form is how to communicate your emotion while working in all the references to the object. Once you have been assigned an object, start thinking about what you associate with that object. What pops into your mind first? As you practice this form, vary your approach. See how people react when you make simple references. See how it goes when you adopt a more subtle point of view.

Don't be afraid to actually state the object's name in your opening line. It's not always necessary but often helps. In fact, the conductor can take a role in this. If you begin your rant and after a while the conductor's still unsure what your object assignment was, the conductor should continue pointing at you. When it feels to the student like their turn is longer than usual, that's because the conductor is trying to communicate to you that it's unclear what your object is. In the next few moments you should flat-out state what it is. Yes, this begs the question of how astute the conductor is at making this call. You, as the performer, may feel that you've very cleverly been ranting and it's not necessary to say the object's name. The best arbiter of whether the conductor has a good ear for this point is how the audience is reacting. If the performer is going on and the audience is reacting strongly then it's a good sign that they know what the object is.

After the first pass the conductor will work the middle, which is to say that he's going to give the people other than those two on the ends of the line a chance for a second rant. It's good to make it seem like you're bouncing around a bit, even though it's an orchestrated randomness and winds up in the middle. So in the first pass of seven people you go to their positions in the order of 1-2-3-4-5-6-7. For the second pass, try going 2-5-3-6-4. Whatever order is selected, when you are doing the form in performance, rehearse it with the students beforehand so that they are ready to go when the time comes. You don't have to remember the entire order, just who you come after on that second pass. But be ready in case the conductor forgets the order and comes to you sooner than expected.

After this second round all except the two people on the end have gone twice. Next comes "the zipper."

The conductor has to make a call while the second round is going on. That call is which one of the two people on the ends has the (potentially) funnier assigned emotion-object. The choice usually gets made based on who seems to have done the most with what they were assigned during the first pass. The person chosen will be the one the conductor will go to after the center person gets their shot at the end of round two. Your end people need to be especially good at the form because this is something you cannot predetermine – both have to be ready for the conductor to go to them.

The conductor goes to one of the two end people. They do their second rant. When the conductor's ready to point to the person at the other end – after all, everybody else has now gone twice so now it's that person's turn – the conductor doesn't just point to that person. Instead, they move their hand, a wafting gesture if you will, from the end person who's been ranting, past the faces of the performers between the two ends, until ultimately arriving at the person on the other end. This movement from one side to the other is the zipper. When the conductor's hand passes in front of the face of the students between the two end people, they should make a few sounds in that brief moment – it doesn't even have to be intelligible. The effect you're trying to achieve is akin to when you would spin the tuning dial on an old fashioned radio – you hear little blasts of sounds from the other stations as you move from the first to your destination.

So now the conductor's pointing at the person of the other end of the line and that person is doing their rant. Everybody's had the chance to go twice. Now what? ***ZIPPER BACK!*** The conductor simply does the same hand wafting movement back to the other end and we get another blast of that old-time radio effect. Now we've returned to the other end person, and (a-ha!) that person has to now provide a third rant related to their emotion-object. That's why the conductor had to make that choice about which one of the end people seemed to be doing the best with their assignment – that person has to begin and end the zipper.

The next move for the conductor is to bring the form to its grand finale. When the zip is done, both performers and conductor know that the finale is coming next. The conductor will stop pointing at the end person, ending their rant. Then the conductor waves both arms above his head in broad circles, and the performers all talk. It's fine if they say something related to their assignment, but it's not absolutely necessary as their talking over one another will make all sound a blur to the audience. The conductor dramatically stops the arms-circling and brings his hands down to his side which is the cue for the orchestra to be silent. Now it is time for the big ending moment. The conductor quickly points to one last person and they deliver the final line.

Keep it short and sweet (and funny, please). The student selected for that last line should be someone other than the person on the end who's already had to give three rants because they began and ended the zipper. It looks better to the viewing audience and it would be unfair to put someone in the position of possibly having to come up with a fourth interesting/comedic rant on their assignment.

The students should keep in mind that this is a stand-alone form, so you can be a bit more scatological, profane or gratuitously mayhem-oriented if you like than you would be in performing a scene.

One additional nice touch: when you get to the end of the second round, the conductor is pointing to the performer in the center. The conductor lets that person do their rant, but towards the end, and before initiating the zipper, he begins moving his pointing hand back and forth between the center person and the ones on either side. All three should be ranting given this cue. Then the conductor raises the pointing hand even higher while waving it to and fro and all three begin ranting progressively louder. Then the conductor begins lowering the waving hand and all three begin lowering their voice. When they're at a whisper, it's time to begin the zipper. Again, it is swell if all three are ranting on point concerning their assigned emotion/object, but it's okay if they're not. This is more for effect than content.

42. A to Z 90

Students alternate lines of dialogue in a scene that cannot be longer than 90 seconds. The first line must begin with a word starting with the letter "A," the second line begins with a word that begins with the letter "B" and so on. The scene ends when they reach the 26th line – the "Z" word line – or when time runs out.

Two students start onstage and ask for a song title to inspire what the scene is about. In performance, they should explain to the audience: "We're about to play a scene in which we will exchange single lines of dialogue. The catch being that the first word of the first line of dialogue has to begin with the letter "A," the next line begins with a word that starts with the letter "B," and so on. The scene is over when we get to the "Z" line or when time expires, because we've only got 90 seconds to play the scene." The performers note that the clock only starts when the first line is spoken. This allows the scene's initiator to begin with as much spacework as they like since it won't count against their 90 seconds.

A nice trick to employ when starting is to use names to take care of a couple of the early letters.

"**A**ndrea, we need to talk about your spending," followed by "**B**ob, stop hassling me about buying mink pants."

As with any scene, it's always important that the storyline is clear within the first 3-5 exchanges of dialogue. You will need to pack a lot of info into the first few lines of dialogue.

The who-what-where of the scene is established early on. Now another time-saving trick can be employed. When you get to the middle of the alphabet, use a spate of short, even single-word, sentences so that you can cover ground and move the story along.

"**M**aybe later we should go."

"**N**ow!"

"**O**kay."

"**P**lease hand me the keys."

"**Q**uick, let's get to the car."

During the improv, when you've said your line and are listening for the response you are fully expecting that your scene partner will "hit their mark" and begin their line with a word that starts with the next letter of the alphabet. So while you're listening to their line you are also repeating to yourself what your next letter of the alphabet is. This helps condition you to remember to start your next line correctly. Let's say though, that your scene partner blows their line. If they skip ahead just one letter or so, the best thing to do is to adjust and continue on from there. Do not worry about the letter(s) skipped. It puts you on the spot, because you were all prepared to do a certain letter for your first word. With practice of the form, you should be able to cover these errors seamlessly. Again, we are reminded of how important it is for the improviser to be flexible as they play the scene.

However, if your partner goes so far off base that someone wants to call the Military Police - starting a sentence with a "Y" word when they should be providing a "G" word - then you should go to the letter that your scene partner should have gone to. They should be practiced enough to recognize their error, pick up on what you are doing and resume the scene from there.

Students have to guard against the little personal vocal habits we all unconsciously fall into. You can very absent-mindedly throw in an "ah," "uhm," or "y'know" at the start of dialogue. It's generally not going to be a problem for you, except that in this form it violates the rules of the game. So if you find yourself liable to falling in one of these habits, you must focus harder when playing this improv.

Some tricks are done for effect on the audience. One is to use an "ex-"starting word (exactly, extremely, exit) when you get to the letter "X." Another is to use the word "you" when you are the letter "U." Students have to treat the words like you are at the letter "X" or "U" though and proceed from there. Both people playing the improv should be similarly skilled so they are ready to deal with one of these tricks being pulled.

The input you receive of song title is just to get you inspired about the who, what OR where of the scene. It doesn't have to be an influence for all three elements. If you find a way to have it influence all three, that's great, but just know it's not a requirement. Similarly, if there is a popular music video for the song you don't have to make the scene a parody of that video. Remember, the initiator makes the connection to the suggestion. The other person simply follows their lead and is only concerned with making a good scene and obeying the given constraints of this game.

The person keeping track of the time should call out when there is 30 seconds left and, again, when 10 seconds are left. Not only does that give the students a sense of whether they're going to make it to "Z" or not, but it heightens the audience's anticipation. In performance situations, the person on the lights should also be on their toes. They need to kill the lights when the person tracking time calls "Blackout." Often, the person running the lights is the one tracking time. Feel free to fudge a bit and give the students a couple extra seconds if they are on the cusp of reaching the "Z" line. (Blackout also occurs when they reach the "Z" word line before their 90 seconds are up.)

A great scene which only gets to the letter "S" before the lights blackout is better than a so-so scene that hits the "Z" line in under a minute. Again we're reminded that you do not surrender the scene to the game. The story of the scene is what matters most. The story must keep making sense in the context of what's already been established. The performers should never say/do something just for the sake of satisfying the requirement of the game being played.

Good "Z" words to end with are "Zoinks!" and "Zowie!" or "Zeus Almighty!" — as far as the audience is concerned they work in any situation. Usually an audience is going to be awed by your ability to go thru the alphabet correctly. You really wow them by making the scene memorable.

43. DATING GAME

One student tries to guess the emotion and profession assigned to three other students by playing a game that parodies the classic TV game show The Dating Game.

This is great for class and is also a very popular performance piece.

This game requires five students: a host, the eligible bachelor or bachelorette, and three people of the opposite sex to play their potential date. For the following explanation, let's say this performance is with a bachelorette and three eligible bachelors. There's a male host.

The student playing the bachelorette is encouraged to play a character she's been working on in advance. For example, Anne did brilliant takes on Laura Bush, Martha Stewart and Kathy Griffin. When she chose to do one of those characters in this form, she would inform the host so that he could introduce her appropriately. Playing a set character is encouraged because there's a point in the game where the bachelorette gets to introduce her character to the audience. Little touches like this greatly enhance the audience appreciation for what's going on.

The host can also play someone well known, perhaps for their romantic trials and tribulations. The host could also play a generic game-show host character if that's the way they want to go. The point is, the host should also come to the form having prepared something specific.

You will find that with many performance-oriented pieces there are aspects which can be prepared in advance. This preparation gives the piece a polish which enhances its enjoyment by the audience.

The host introduces the piece to the audience while setting three chairs next to one another. He then places a fourth downstage left and facing away from the first three. The conceit being maintained by the players is that the bachelorette cannot see the bachelors. In fact, the bachelorette is encouraged to shoot a glance their way during the game to pick up some clues about their assignment by their physical actions. With practice the bachelorette develops a sense for when to sneak that peak.

The host makes his introduction:

HOST: "Welcome everyone to that great game show of the '60s and '70s, *The Dating Game*. I'm your host, <whomever you want to play>, and let's introduce our lovely bachelorette, Miss <name>. All right young lady, please head out to the isolation booth (she exits the room). Now let's welcome our three eligible bachelors."

The three dudes enter and take seats at the chairs grouped together. (Remember, you could also play the game with three bachelorettes and an eligible bachelor.)

HOST: "Okay audience, to get things started we need three professions for these lucky fellows."

Let's say they get Cop, Lawyer and, as invariably occurs, Proctologist. Usually the host lets these be assigned stage right to stage left. To make sure that the players know what they've been given, he should tap them on the shoulder as the assignments are called out. (If you think you're getting a particular suggestion too often, like Proctologist, you can prevent it being given by asking the audience "May we have the names of three professions, but not proctologist, since we always get that." Just don't be shocked if they then substitute gynecologist.)

Then the host asks the audience for emotions or "states of being." A "state of being" could be "French," "spiritual," "penniless," etc. The host should randomly assign what the audience calls out to the players so as to prevent the audience controlling what gets matched up, and to some extent prevent them from realizing what's been assigned to whom, because we're about to remind them anyway.

Then the host says how he's about to let the bachelorette back in but first the bachelors will remind the audience of their assignments.

The bachelors don't just say their assigned emotion/profession. They always start with "I'm a" as in "I'm a French Proctologist." Remember, you need to have the mindset that you're not *playing at* being the character, you are the character. As Barbara Walters once famously asked "If you were a tree what kind of tree would you be?" It wasn't what kind of tree would you play. By starting with "I'm a..." you are reinforcing this concept.

Once all three have reminded the audience of their assignments we bring the bachelorette back in. The host invites her to say a little about herself. This is the performer's chance to introduce herself to the audience as the character she's chosen. The character can be completely made up or be an impression of a celebrity, and don't be shy about the person you choose not being super-famous. As mentioned, Anne did a killer Kathy Griffin during the first season of Griffin's "D-List" reality show.

Once the bachelorette finishes her introductory speech, the host cues her that it's time to get to the game. "Well that sounds great, but let's get to the game now. You know how we play, so first question please."

The questions are always the same and asked in the same order. You don't just wing it when it comes to what questions you ask. The questions, and their order, always being the same allow the bachelors a chance to prepare their responses while the host is introducing the bachelorette. The bachelors always respond in the same order, from the one sitting closest to the bachelorette to the one furthest away. So as soon as they know their assigned emotion/profession they are preparing what they are going to say and refining it.

These are the questions we use. You can change them to whatever you like, if you think it will better serve the form. The first question is "What's your idea of romance?" then "What's your favorite film?" followed by "Where do you see yourself in five years?"

When answering the questions, the bachelors are balancing charming the audience against giving clues to the bachelorette about their assignment. So as soon as they know their emotion/profession, they pretty much tune out everything else being said as they consider how they will respond to the questions they know are coming.

During the first round of replies, the bachelors should be less concerned with giving the bachelorette clues than charming the audience with their reply. There are clues for the bachelorette in their response but they should not be obvious. The first question is intentionally a very open-ended question so that their answer can take many different paths. The bachelors know the audience knows their assignment. The clues contained in their reply to the first question can therefore be geared more towards getting a reaction from the audience than giving the bachelorette clues about their character.

In responding, the bachelors are thinking of key words associated with their assigned profession, and are striving to work them into their response in a way that connects with the audience without just flat-out giving away their assignment to the bachelorette.

For example, if you're a French Proctologist, you might respond to the first question, in your best bad French accent, "I think that we would make beautiful music together as we head out for my favorite bar, Monsieur Brown's. Because I am a gentleman, when we arrive, I will pull out your stool for you."

If the profession is mapmaker, you might talk about taking your date to a favored Italian restaurant, Vespucci's, because you know, and are hoping that at least a few people in the audience will also, that Amerigo Vespucci is the mapmaker credited for naming America. Don't worry about your clue being too obscure. If at least one or two people get it and start laughing the rest of the audience will join in so that they don't look like they aren't as swift on the uptake as the rest.

What you absolutely have to avoid is the charmless reply which makes it absolutely clear what you've been assigned. If you've been assigned "angry barber" and your first question reply is, angrily, "I'd take you down to my shop, strap you in the chair and shave your head!" well, that's pretty direct, and not very romantic to boot.

Or let's say you are an "angry librarian." If, in a really mean voice, your response to the question about your idea of romance could be "I'd like to get you down in the dusty stacks, near fiction, 3.01, and I'd really like to stamp your library card, if you know what I mean."

The bachelorette would have to be a bit thick not to realize that you are a librarian, so avoid a reply that gives things away right away. Believe it or not, the purpose of the game is not for the bachelorette to be able to successfully guess all the assignments. The purpose is to play the form well – don't surrender the scene to the game.

Since in this first reply, the content of the answer is geared more toward charming the audience with its wit than cluing the bachelorette in, I coach the bachelorette to pay more attention to the possible emotion, state-of-being assignment during this first round. While the bachelors are striving to be subtle in the content of their response they have carte blanche to ham it up as much as they want when it comes to getting across the emotion/state-of-being assignment.

The trouble with some emotions/state-of-beings is that they cannot be acted out as much as talked about (i.e., cheap) so the bachelorette has to be aware that it's possible that the dialogue may contain clues to the emotion as well as the profession. It's fairly easy to pick up on this happening because the bachelor seems pretty even-keel as they deliver their reply. So, the bachelorette should realize that the emotion/state-of-being clues are also in the dialogue.

It's so important that the bachelors charm the audience with their first reply because then the audience will "forgive" them virtually announcing their assignment when they respond to the subsequent questions. You are prohibited from saying "policeman" if assigned that noble profession. However, you can say just about any synonym to it in round two or three if your first round reply has won the audience over.

When responding to the second question ("What's your favorite film?") it's okay to say you prefer books or TV. Sometimes you want to do this because it serves you better in giving the clue you want.

When someone's been assigned fireman, they invariably respond with *Backdraft* as their favorite movie. You can understand why your first response being clever is so important since the subsequent questions may have less latitude for charming clue-giving.

If you're ever given the emotional assignment "horny" then in addition to whatever film title you give for your profession you add a few special ones. For a horny fireman, and what fireman isn't, you might respond "My favorite film is *Backdraft*....oh and *Debbie Does Dallas, Misty Beethoven,* and *Gentlemen Prefer Ginger.*" This "works," which is to say that it will get a reaction from the audience.

Whenever you're responding, you cannot say any of the words comprising your emotion/profession assignment. So if you are an apathetic golf caddy, and who isn't, and you're asked what your favorite film is, you can't say *Caddy Shack* but you can talk about how much you like that film where Bill Murray plays that goofy groundskeeper ("18th hole of the Masters....Cinderella story...") who's at war with the gopher but you just cannot remember the title. The bachelorette may not know the title, but they have to know that the reason you cannot say the title is that it's part of what you've been assigned. This may help them when it comes time to guess.

When responding to the question about where you see yourself in five years, you should think in terms of what would be a promotion, or a career progression, for your character. If you've been assigned "depressed magician" you might respond, "Well, if I haven't disappeared from life's stage by then, I'd like to run a retirement home for performing rabbits and pigeons."

Once all three rounds of question/answers are complete, the host prompts the bachelorette to guess.

HOST: "All right bachelorette, who's it going to be? Bachelor #1, Mike G? Bachelor #2, Dave K? Or Bachelor #3, Errol G?" (The host substitutes the bachelors' actual names.)

The bachelorette eventually selects the bachelor whose assignment she is most certain of. First, though, she dismisses the bachelors in order of who she is least sure of. It's really important that the last thing she says in dismissing each of them is her guess at their emotion/assignment. "I really enjoyed meeting bachelor number one but I can't see myself dating a clumsy pastry chef." What you never want to do is bury the punchline, which means putting the punchline in the middle of the response. Here, the punchline is your guess of the emotion/assignment. You wouldn't want to say "I cannot see myself with Bachelor # 1 because a clumsy pastry chef is really not the kind of guy who I'd really like to be dating."

The bachelorette understands that it's not so important that they get it right as they are decisive when making their guesses. A wrong guess about emotion/profession is just as funny, and sometimes funnier, than a right guess. Admittedly, you are hoping that your final selection is correct because that's the one you are most confident in. It's nice if the final pick is a right guess, but believe me, a wrong guess, honestly made, will get at least as big a response.

The bachelorette must also keep in mind when guessing that it's got to be an emotion and a profession. Guessing "timid jogger" is not so great and the host has free reign to comment on how there's not so much money to be made in jogging these days.

For their part, the bachelors can acknowledge a correct guess, or GENTLY correct a wrong one as they either depart the stage or embrace the bachelorette after being selected. If you were a clumsy pastry chef and she guesses timid jogger when dismissing you, you could say something like "Well I am a timid jogger but I try to make ends meet as a pastry chef, albeit clumsy." If the bachelorette guesses an emotion that is in the right area but perhaps not exactly it, do not correct her.

Although guys play guys and gals play gals in our shows, in one performance we were short-handed. We had a bachelor interviewing three women and I had to play the third bachelorette, named Pat. We explained to the audience that it seems that name caused an error by the game show's casting department and the character was just being a good sport. Hilarity ensued. Trust me. Furthermore, you can play a same-sex version of the form, not that there's anything wrong with that.

The questions do not have to be set in stone. Whatever you choose, it's sticking to the order that you've decided on that matters. One night – and none since, because I keep making a point of it in rehearsal – our bachelorette screwed up by asking a new question first and then asking the first question second. And guess who was sitting in the first bachelor's spot? I'd like to be able to report that I stammered out lengthy answers in order to buy time for the other two guys to figure out what they were going to say, but mainly I was thinking homicidal thoughts while cobbling together a reply.

44. SIXTY SECONDS

A 60 seconds-long scene is played. It is then replayed in its entirety, but in successively shorter versions of 30, 15, 7.5 and 1 seconds.

This form, which is also great in performance, requires at least five students: One to host, two to start onstage and two others offstage who will join the scene at some point.

The host asks for a location which could fit on the stage. The host then explains that the students will play a scene set at the location and that the scene will be exactly sixty seconds long. The host tells the audience that the clock won't start until the first line of dialogue is spoken, permitting the initiator to begin with all the spacework they want. Although they've been given the location, if it feels generic ("bar") you might want to make it as specific as a Philadelphia tavern on July 4, 1776.

The scene begins. The students offstage should give the pair onstage 20-30 seconds to establish the storyline before they enter. They don't have to enter together but can come in separately.

When a minute has gone by the host calls the blackout. Then she explains that the students will repeat the scene but in half the time - 30 seconds. They will cover all the ground they did in the original scene, just quicker.

The students play the scene. The host calls blackout at 30 seconds. Then the host announces that the scene will be played in 15 seconds. After that version the students will play it all in 7.5 seconds and finally they play the scene in 1 second.

When doing the 30-second version of the scene, the goal is to be as faithful as possible to story of the 60 second version. You don't change anything in the story; you just try and do it twice as fast. First of all, it develops skill for the performers because it requires discipline to repeat everything in order. It's also important for the audience's sake – it gives them a chance to follow the flow of what you're doing. Plus, it sets them up for any changes you make to the scene when you do the 15 or 7.5 second version. During these versions you do want to insert a surprising change. Just don't change too much; you still want the scene to be fairly faithful to its original take. The final, 1 second scene is a simple shout out of the most important line you had during the scene.

As I mentioned in the introduction, my improv troupe *KLAATU* began performing in 1998, and in one of our initial shows we were playing this form. I was one of the two starting performers; the other was Dana. There were two other females waiting offstage to join in, Denise and Kathy. The host was Craig. He asked for a location that could fit on the stage. Someone called out "Israel" and he took it!

This was the first in a series of mistakes made in the playing of the scene; most of them by yours truly, but the scene came off very well, proving one of the theories in the great book on Improvisation, *Truth in Comedy*, which argues that there are no mistakes made onstage, just opportunities for something wonderful to occur. The wonderful happens by working your way through the error(s). You do this by trying to make sense of, to justify, something which seems not to fit.

We start and Dana initiates the scene and establishes she's a flight attendant on an El-Al flight. So, of course, I figure I should be an Arab terrorist hijacking the plane. This is mistake #2, because I started us off playing characters who are strangers to one another.

Eventually Denise and Kathy join the scene as airline security agents and I ask "Why are there no men on this flight?" Here is mistake #3: don't ask questions onstage. So the scene moves to its conclusion where I'm offered a bagel by the attendant, take a bite and spit it out, exclaiming "I spit this out of my mouth" – when you're unsure what to say, state the obvious. Then we do our faster versions at 30 and 15 seconds without really changing anything. Now it's time for the 7.5 second version. With only 7.5 seconds to do the scene, if you are going to cover it from beginning to end you've got to haul booty, and one of the best ways to do so is to combine dialogue, distilling it to its essence, compressing the storyline.

During the initial 60 second scene I asked "Why are there no men on this flight?" and Denise responded, "I'm a man." This was mistake #4. Don't deny what other characters are establishing. If there are no men on the flight, you're a woman. But this led to funny, snarky exchanges during the 30 and 15 second versions, like "You're my kind of man," etc. Now at the 7.5 second version we race to the moment where I ask the question, but instead of asking it, I just whip my head in her direction and say "What are you, a man?" I know it's one of those you-had-to-be-there moments but it really caught the audience off guard and got a great response. They were conditioned to my asking the question at that point and hearing her response; because we had such little time, I simply compressed the exchange into a single line of dialogue.

Now, you might be asking about how it's possible to do a scene about planes being hijacked by terrorists. This scene was done in 1998, well before 9/11. It does, though, beg the question of what content should and should not be attempted onstage.

Pythagoras had his mathematical theorems. Woody Allen has his formula for humor: Tragedy + Time = Comedy.

This means that if enough time has gone by, however tragic the event was, it can be used for comic purposes. In performance we have done incredibly well-received scenes about the Lincoln assassination and the sinking of the Titanic. To some extent there are certain ways to approach scenes about the Kennedy assassination which can "work." But we've yet to do a 9/11 scene and I don't intend on doing one in my lifetime. Believe me; it's okay to reject an audience suggestion.

Here's another example of how a small change can have a big impact. In one performance, two guys are at a peep show – Edgar and Kevin. They're having a grand old time when Cindy, Kevin's wife, shows up. Edgar starts telling her to leave Kevin alone and let him have some fun. Kevin suddenly takes umbrage at Edgar telling his wife what to do, so he takes a swing at him – punch-throwing in improv is serious business; you need to make direct eye contact with the other person and throw the punch in semi-slow motion and throw it in a way that intends to miss the target by a good foot. So Kevin's character decks Edgar, who does a controlled, slow-motion fall to the stage floor. They repeat this for the 30 second version, but when the 15 second version comes around, instead of decking Edgar, Kevin decks his wife, Cindy's character. Kevin, having already made eye-contact already with Cindy can pull this off. It was a great and completely unexpected adjustment to the flow of the scene.

Like many performance pieces, the host should be encouraged to play a character. When *The Apprentice* was first airing, and especially since we were performing in NYC, I would host the form as Donald Trump, occasionally adding one of the cast members to play one of his aide-de-camps. Just as often I would play Yul Brynner, which might seem like an obscure choice, but between the accent and riffing off movies he'd been in when commenting on the scenes just played – "I have not witnessed scene-stealing like that since Steve McQueen in *The Magnificent Seven*" – it worked. Personally, I think Yul still resonates because of the annual airing of one of the greatest movies ever made, *The Ten Commandments*, which I happen think is also one of the funniest films ever made due to the corny dialogue.

45. POET'S CORNER

In this form students improvise poetry in styles chosen in advance.

We usually have a host and three poets; I wouldn't suggest doing it with any fewer; nor would I suggest more than five poets. There will be two rounds of poetry and the poets play the same characters each round.

One student serves as host of an evening of the finest improvisational poetry. They should choose to be playing a character from their repertoire, perhaps a celebrity impersonation.

It's always good to make the venue specific. In our performances we always act like it's the 92nd Street Y, because in New York City this is the venue where a number of excellent speakers are presented throughout the year.

The host welcomes the audience to the venue and asks for a topic the poets can expound upon. They repeat the topic that's been given back to the audience to make sure that everyone's heard it, especially the poets.

The host then rambles on an UNRELATED topic for about 20-30 seconds to give the poets a chance to collect their thoughts. Then, in a pre-determined order, they come forward and deliver their poems, referencing the suggestion in some way.

The host then gets a second suggestion, and again expounds on something unrelated for 20-30 seconds to give the poets a chance to think about what they'll do. Then, in the same order and playing the same character, the poets do a second round of poetry.

Some great poet styles we have seen used in the troupe include:

Traditional: poets choose recognizable styles, including limerick, rhyming couplet and haiku. Often they choose to match the style to a certain character. I do a poet who is a one-eyed, angry ex-con with a predilection for haiku.

Character: a number of people find their character first and then figure out a style. We have had cheerleader poets, singing poets and celebrity poets (my Jimmy Stewart poet begins each poem with "I had a dog whose name was Bo").

Punchline driven: We had a great improviser, Caprice, who did a suicidal poet, kind of 'Night Mother meets Sylvia Plath, and each poem ended with her setting herself up for peril and ending with her shouting "so that I can die! Die! Die!" (It also serves as an excellent example of how to take a very serious, sensitive subject and exaggerate it for comic effect.)

Remember that it's okay if nobody gets how your poem connects to the suggestion as long as you know what the connection is. Someone in the audience will likely get it and the rest will act as if they do so they don't feel out of step. You don't want to make a habit of it being too obtuse – lest you seem like *The Shawshank Redemption*'s warden – because you do want the audience to follow your line of thought.

The poem should be working its way toward a significant ending; a punchline if you will. What you have to watch out for is telegraphing where you are headed. If the suggestion is hair, try to avoid an ending that's easy to see coming:
"so like Britney Spears in her barber's chair,
  I decided to shave off my hair!"

Often it's best to use the topic early in the poem and work toward a surprising ending:
"I decided to shave off my hair,
  Just like Britney Spears in her barber's chair."

Also, you can get away with not quite using the suggestion, as in the case where we got "butter" from the audience and I did my Jimmy Stewart:

"I had a dog whose name was Bo,
He lived a life of leisure, eating at whim you know.
He got real fat with such flabby skin
That we put him on a diet of margarine."

No, it's not exactly Robert Frost, but it surprised the audience by taking them from the "butter" suggestion to "margarine."

Another fun technique is to make the audience think you're heading to an ending where the rhyming word that's coming up is R-rated, but instead you plop in a totally non-rhyming word.

"life had me down on my luck,
 So all I said was what the for-Pete's-sake"

A few other things to keep in mind:
- Everyone performing knows what style everyone else is using so that there is no repetition.
- Stay in the same order. The idea is to let those who are best go towards the end. It's also good to identify someone who's adept at going first, especially to guard against the host forgetting to do their bit to buy the other poets time.

- Another reason for the order being based on who's adept at the form is that you need to avoid poems similar in concept. If you have an idea based on the topic, and someone going ahead of you does something similar, then you have to change. So, if you're not going first you have to think about what you're going to do and also have a Plan B, an alternate poem, just in case..
- This form is a "stand-alone" which is to say that you're not building a scene, so you have greater latitude in the content you choose and how over-the-top you play it. You can, if you choose, be a bit more scatological, profane, etc because what you do is independent of what the other poets are doing. (Just remember that it's not the goal to be profane, scatological, etc.)
- PROPS! This is a form where you can use costumes or props to help convey your character. Although in scene work we only use imaginary props, here you know what your character will be from the get go, so a little dressing-up the part polishes the form. Be sure to consider what forms you might be doing before/after this to consider

whether you have time to do any elaborate changes.
- How do you get to Carnegie Hall? Practice! Practice! Practice your poetry styles between classes or performances. Consider the nuances you might add to your poet character. If your character's form is haiku, you can get away with something that sort of seems like a haiku. However, your goal should be to actually improvise a haiku each time out, so learn the form and its requirements. You will wow every English major in the audience.
- The host should be playing a specific character, too. Also, think in terms of a funny/topical closing line – "See you next week, when the President explains why his crummy approval ratings really don't matter."

46. SEVEN-MINUTE STORY

A story is told via a series of scenes played out over seven minutes by all the performers.

This is a great performance piece.

Start with everyone upstage. Two performers who were designated beforehand step forward. They ask for an input (we usually ask for a problem that people can face). Then they explain that they will use the suggestion as the basis for a story they will tell via a series of scenes to be played out over the next seven minutes. The two then fall into scene-initiation mode. One eventually taps the other and becomes the initiator, the other becomes the supporter.

At some point in the scene one of two things must happen. Either one of the other performers upstage will enter the scene or one of them will signal that they want to change to the next scene of the story.

We know that if they are joining the scene they must enter appropriately. If the scene is taking place indoors, is it appropriate for them to enter without knocking? Perhaps they are part of the family unit or live there. Otherwise…they knock. Either way, their first line will inform the other players in the scene about who their character is. They should already know at least one other character in the scene. They are also joining the scene to help move the story along, so they need to have an agenda for their character's entrance. You're not just wandering in for the sake of getting stage time. The instructor should be taking note of what people entering are bringing to the story.

Once someone establishes a character during the scene, then that's the character they will play for the duration of the story. Keep in mind how characters, just like people, have public and private roles. The postman character delivering the mail in the first scene can also be revealed to be the husband of another character in a later scene.

In theory, everyone could join the first scene before the next scene begins.

If, rather than joining the ongoing scene, someone upstage has an idea for the next scene in the story, they initiate it by doing a gentle trot down one side of the stage, around and in front of the performers playing the scene and to the other side of the stage. This cues everyone that the current scene is over and they should retreat upstage, assuming a neutral position. It is "neutral" in the sense that they are not in character mode, but are waiting to resume their established character at some point. In performance an audience will always pick up on this theatrical conceit, realizing when actors are "onstage" and not.

After doing the run-around, that performer must initiate the next scene. They point to at least one of the people upstage to signal that they want them to start the next scene with them – perhaps it's someone with an established character or else it's someone who has not established their character in the story yet. They start the scene; the next part of the story. The scene goes on and either people join in or someone begins the next scene.

Perhaps the initiator of that scene selected someone who had already established a character. The instructor should fault an initiator if they select someone who has established a character and then seems to want them to play a "new" character. Similarly, the instructor watches out for people who "forget" the character they established earlier. They have forgotten the rules of the game.

Although the performers keep playing their established character, you can pull a bit of double duty by joining a scene to play a non-character role because it's what the scene seems to need. For example: furniture in an apartment (i.e., a lamp), or a tree, or a forest animal.

Keep in mind that it is possible for characters to be differently related to others in the scene. The police officer we see in scene one may later turn out to also be the mother of a character established in scene two.

Remember to keep thinking in "small town / big hell" terms. It helps explain how the characters all know one another. Every character must know at least one other character on some level.

The instructor will call out "one minute" at about the six minute point. This indicates that there is ABOUT one minute left to go. At that point there will be a scene going on. Ideally this scene will give way to the concluding scene of the story. It is okay if the scene being played when the cue is given turns out to be the final scene. What you do not want to have happen is for there to be multiple scenes being crammed into the last minute. Usually the development of the story has identified a couple of characters as central figures. We usually want these characters to be in the final scene to help resolve the story.

After hearing the "one minute" cue, the person running the lights will black them out anywhere from 45 to 75 seconds later. Yes, we're fudging a bit. Believe me, in performance there is nobody in the audience timing you – they're watching the scene. The person running the lights and doing the blackout is looking for a strong moment (also known as "a button") in which to end the scene. It's up to the performers to provide one. That's why you get the cue that there's a minute left. Work on getting to the story's end! In a class, the instructor can do this by letting the final scene play out, however long it takes. Then they discuss it with the students, pointing out possible alternate choices and the amount of time they took. It is a good idea to "rewind" the story and let the students play out the revised version of the final scene.

When a scene is going on, it may be joined by as many people who want to join in. However, you should only initiate scenes from the "neutral" upstage position. You should not do it from within the scene being played. If you are in the scene and have an idea for what the next scene should be, find a justifiable way to exit the scene. Make your exit. Get to the upstage position and then do the run-around. If you cannot accomplish this smoothly, then you have to let someone else initiate the next scene.

In choosing what the next scene should be about, keep in mind that time is limited. If the first three scenes concentrate on a central storyline and specific characters, it's generally not going to work out if the fourth scene tries to bring a new storyline, a new thread, into play because there's just not enough time to draw the storylines together. Scenes should be 30-60 seconds and should get right to the point – what's the key piece of information that the initiator thinks should be brought out by the scene?

To help "cover ground" in the story it's possible for the dialogue in a scene to suggest how events have occurred between scenes. For example, the first scene can be about the end of a couple's first date. The next scene can find them already married following a whirlwind romance. We don't need to see the wedding! (For my money, whirlwind is anything under five years.) The brilliant AMC series *Mad Men* is an example of important activity occurring between episodes, like Roger's remarriage and Joan's wedding.

The form's seven minutes length is not sacrosanct – anywhere from five to ten minutes is good for performances. In class, I sometimes use the rule of thumb that the length should be N-1 minutes, where N is the number of students performing. We have also done up to 30 minute stories. They've been great fun, even when the story seems to be going nowhere, because the students show a remarkable propensity for getting things back on track. Give it a try!

47. SUPERHERO EULOGY

Performers come forward one-by-one to deliver the eulogy of a superhero.

This is another form which can be used in performance. It works best with a host and three players. (You can use up to five people, as we sometimes do to give stage time to additional cast members.)

Three students stand facing the audience. Between them, center stage, is a table or even a chair. The host stands beside the table and is holding an "urn" behind their back – this is a form where it's okay to use an actual prop for the urn. The host somberly asks the audience for the suggestion of an object. Let's say she gets "rake."

The host, while placing the urn on the table, explains to the audience that those standing behind her are here to perform a eulogy. Use words to the effect "We are gathered here tonight to pay our final respects to our superhero friend, Rake-man. Rake-man was a much admired and beloved member of our community and, as such, will be sorely missed in the years to come. So it's only fitting that we have gathered here tonight to pay our final respects to our superhero friend, Rake-man."

One-by-one those standing step forward and deliver their eulogy.

The order in which they come up is totally at their discretion. Ideally, each subsequent eulogy will be funnier than that preceding so that the best comes last. But since there's no communication among the performers, how can this occur?

As soon as the object is named, the performers start thinking about what they're going to say. They ignore the instructor's spiel to the audience about this being a "superhero eulogy" – the point of the spiel is to buy them time so they can decide what they'll say.

How to decide what to say? There are two steps to the process. First, think of things you associate with the object. That's got to be the basis for what's funny in your eulogy. Second, there's a reason we've made it a *superhero* eulogy. Part of what you say in your eulogy should be informed by the comic book ethos. Are you the superhero ally of Rake-man; his arch-nemesis; his sidekick or love interest? Furthermore, what is it that led to Rake-man's death? What are the ramifications of his now sleeping the big sleep?

So each person comes to their decision. Now, to return to the initial question, how do we try to work it so the best comes last? The way to try and make this happen is for each performer to make a judgment call on how funny their bit is. If you think it will "kill," then hang back for a while and try to let the others go first.

There's a risk to this, though. What if you're hanging back and someone you let go ahead of you does something similar to what you were planning to do? Then you have to do something different. So if you are bold enough to hang back for the sake of the performance coming off better, then you have to have an alternate thing to do, a "plan B" ready.

On the flip side, let's say you think you've got something great and you're hanging back. But nobody is going. Does everyone think they've got something great? Does everybody else have nothing? Is it a mix? Well, if nobody's going then feel free to take your killer eulogy right on up there. For the sake of the flow of the form you do not want to have long pauses before getting started or between the eulogies.

The instructor watches out for someone who always goes last because they think that their eulogy is the best but they are invariably mistaken. You must straighten them out.

Conversely, what if you're stymied? You've got the object but you've got nothing. It's a bit of a cheat – which always means that it is a cheat – but you can do a eulogy for someone famous who just passed and then realize that you're in the wrong service. Whatever you do, don't panic, but when you sense you've got nothing you do try and get up there first and say your piece so that you're out of the way.

For presentation purposes, it is extremely helpful for the eulogizer to have a specific character in mind for themselves with very big, character-driven movements as they step up to do their thing. One time the suggestion was "flashing lights" so our superhero was "Flashing Lights Man." Edgar, a member of the troupe, came up to eulogize very stiffed-legged, almost as if his legs were a pole, and holding his arms above his head as if he were balancing an imaginary box. He arrived at the urn, shouted "POP!" and did a 360 degree turn. His first line was "Flashing Lights Man, this is Flash-Cube Man." It was a very retro choice for those who remember the cameras of the '70s, and very funny.

Most often, the punchline involves a direct reference to the object. "We'll miss you rake-man, but at least we still have your sister, the hoe."

Sometimes the punchline of your eulogy is the announcing of who your superhero or archvillain is. "So farewell Chicken-Salad-Sandwich Man. You never had a chance against me, Salmonella Girl."

Other sources for the punchline are how the superhero met his demise or what's going to be the result of their no longer being on the scene. "Farewell Q-Tip Man, now I, Waxy Buildup Boy, will rule the nation's ear canals!"

Sometimes a good punchline isn't a punchline at all. It can be an absurdly long character name. "Farewell, Diploma Man. It's me, Nerd-who-thinks-asking-out-the-football-captain's-cheerleader-girlfriend-won't-get-back-to-him-but-actually-gets-me-stuffed-in-a-locker...Guy."

It's perfectly okay for our late superhero to be a woman. We used to mix it up in performance, but what I found was that performers were automatically assuming "man" when I had just said it was "woman." This led to some *unintentionally* funny moments onstage when the audience realized the performer had not gotten the gender right. Not good.

You can also control to some extent, what you get by changing what you ask for.

"something found in a garage"

"something bought at the drugstore"

"an object that begins with the letter…"

"an object associated with a holiday." Pick one that's near the show date.

VARIATION: Play a seven-minute story set at a wake, with the urn set up center stage. Before moving to the next scene, the initiator must first offer a eulogy after performing the run-around. This is an example of mixing different forms to increase the challenge to the performers. Always be thinking of ways to tweak improvisations.

48. FIRST-LINE, LAST-LINE, WITH CHANGES

A scene begins and ends with lines of dialogue provided by the audience. During the course of the scene, the performers incorporate styles suggested by the audience.

Two performers begin center stage, with a third person serving as the "caller" off to the side. The caller has no formal performance role in the improv, though on rare occasion they may choose to join in with something. The caller's real job is to explain the form and later help move things along by getting suggestions from the audience. In class, the caller is usually the instructor. There are two more performers standing offstage so that they can see what is established by the spacework performed by the onstage duo. Ultimately they will enter the scene.

The performer stage right asks for "a line of dialogue." Not "a first line of dialogue" just "a line of dialogue." The student on their left asks "May I also have a line of dialogue"; nothing about it being an "ending" line of dialogue. (This matters more in performances of the form than in class work. In performance, you want to surprise the audience by revealing that the two lines provided will begin and end the scene. It's not quite a "Luke, I am your father." surprise, but we do what we can.)

Then the caller begins his spiel. This informs the audience what is about to occur, but also buys time for the two performers onstage to consider their choices for who-what-where. Their choice is influenced by that first line of dialogue.

Let's say that the first line given was "They want you as a new recruit" and the second line given was "I imagine that costs a lot."

The caller's spiel goes something along these lines: "We'll now play a scene for you where the first line of dialogue, to be delivered by either student, MUST be (and cues the performer standing stage right to say "They want you as a new recruit.") Our scene MUST end with the line of dialogue (and cues the performer standing stage left to repeat "I imagine that costs a lot.") During the course of the scene, I'll be freezing the action onstage and coming to you for inputs. I may be asking for things like revelations, playwrights, film styles, TV shows, even singing styles which the performers must immediately and seamlessly work into the scene, a scene which MUST begin with the line of dialogue (cues first performer to repeat "They want you as a new recruit") and MUST end with the line of dialogue (cues other performer for "I imagine that costs a lot.") We take you to a scene."

So the performers start their scene by one tapping the other on the shoulder, signaling they are the initiator, and then starting with spacework. Ultimately they say that first line of dialogue provided by the audience.

The caller makes sure they comply or makes them start again. Make sure they start with exactly with what was given, even if they choose to add on to it. "They want you as a new recruit, Dad" is an okay way to start. "Dad, they want you as a new recruit" is not a legit way to get started – the first line's got to start the same way as the audience gave it.

The caller will usually not ask for a revelation unless the scene has been going on for a bit and it's clear that the students have forgotten to establish something important relating to who-what-where. Sometimes the performers are doing well in this regard, but the caller asks for a revelation because they want the audience to help make it even more specific.

When it comes to the styles requested from the audience, we've found that the best sequence is: playwright, film style, TV show and then to conclude with singing style.

The scene begins and eventually the caller freezes the action. How? He yells "FREEZE" and the performers stop moving and talking; the audience understands what's going on, so don't sweat it. Then he asks for the name of a well-known playwright. I don't want to offend any of you among the literati, but the reason we ask for well-known is not because I've given up on the cast knowing a wide range of dramatists. I want the well-known playwright because it makes for more fun for the audience when the cast nails the style right. Invariably we get Shakespeare, Tennessee Williams or David Mamet. I, being the directing sadist I am, do appreciate, however, the occasional tossing off of Inge or Ionesco, just to watch the cast squirm a bit.

When the performers get the style, the key thing is that they NEVER SURRENDER THE SCENE TO THE GAME! This mantra cuts across all short-form improvs. The most important thing is to continue the good story-building work of the scene. When you ask for a well-known playwright and the audience tosses you

Shakespeare, you don't forget everything you've established to delve into some rehash of Hamlet. You want to continue your story, but just now in a Shakespearean style.

What you are trying to do is to layer the style of the playwright onto the established scene; the established story of the scene begins to move along the lines of one of the themes of the playwright's better-known works, and the style of speech is employed as well.

The scene continues until the caller freezes the action again and asks for a film style. As soon as you get the film style you abandon the playwright style. A lot of times the audience is calling out different styles. Don't be afraid to go for a hybrid. If they call out "kung fu" and "western" then make the students continue the story in the style of "kung-fu western."

The scene continues until the next "Freeze!" when the caller asks for a TV show style. Besides evoking the style of the show, if you haven't given any of the characters in the scene names, although you should have, you can use names associated with the TV show. It's not that you're becoming Elaine from *Seinfeld*; it's just that your character's name happens to be the same.

At the next "Freeze!" the caller says "To conclude our scene" before asking for the style of singing. This reminds the students that they should start working toward the final line of dialogue. It also cues the person running the lights to be ready to blackout the scene. Whatever style of singing you get you have to remember one thing – SING YOUR DIALOGUE! Don't chicken out on this.

The two performers offstage can join the scene at any time, but it's generally best to give the two people starting the scene at least 20-30 seconds to get the story rolling. The two offstage can enter together or separately. The caller should avoid changing styles just as someone is entering the scene. Let them establish their character and what they're bringing to the scene's story before changing styles. Performers are allowed to leave the scene (and they can return if they like) but in over ten years of performance I've yet to see anyone do it. Performers love their stage time.

Sometimes I have assigned a fifth student the role of "safety valve." They enter the final, singing, scene only if they see that the performers seem to have forgotten the last line. They enter, perhaps sing a line or two to establish who they are and then get right to the final line - we don't want them forgetting it, too. We once had a fantastic operatic singer, Monica, in the troupe and so I would designate her to enter during the singing scene and deliver the last line; it didn't matter if those onstage knew it or not.

Keep in mind that even though the performer standing stage right at the beginning gets the first line from the audience, either performer can start the scene using that line. Similarly, any performer in the scene can end it using the last line.

The last line doesn't have to be exactly the same as was given for the lights to be blacked out. Close enough is good enough, though exactly as was given is the ideal.

It's important for the caller to have the right sense of when to freeze the action and get a new input. A good idea is to freeze and change whenever the style being played has gotten a strong response (leave 'em wanting more). It's also okay to have a little fun with the cast. Let's say the audience is asked to provide a playwright and they call out Patrick Marber. If the cast doesn't start playing characters who are in love with people other than their significant others (a la his tremendous play *Closer*) then it's all right for the caller to "Freeze!" the action and ask the audience for *"the name of a playwright that the cast actually knows."*

We were fortunate to have Bob in our troupe during the early years. Bob wrote up a synopsis, a cheat-sheet, if you will, on various playwrights which helped familiarize the cast with the many of the artists we could expect to be given. Perhaps you can get someone to do the same for your group but I encourage performers to do as I have and read as many different playwrights as you can. There are a lot of one-day workshops which attempt to teach you how to play a specific style. If you can find one with a good reputation, then check it out. Here are some of my thoughts on playing different styles to help get you started:

SHAKESPEARE – Avoid making it about ending every word spoken with "-eth." "I wish-eth to take-eth a bath-eth after dinner-eth" isn't so charming. Familiarize yourself with the language. Read some of the bard of Avon! When we get this in performance, I'm always thinking of the line "Were but my horse as quick as your tongue or my sword as sharp." That's a cool line. That's what you want to strive for. The language can make a discussion of the mundane seem important. Also, one of the Shakespearean conceits is a character coming downstage to address the audience, as if the other characters in the scene are frozen. Another piece of advice, often attributed to John Gielgud, is to make clear the emotion behind the words being said.

In college I was fortunate to see *Othello* with James Earl Jones in the title role and Christopher Plummer as Iago – that kind of experience sticks with you, so don't be afraid to indulge in attending a performance.

MAMET – It's not a four-letter-word marathon! Now don't worry, you can get to the cussing, but the clever presentation is to get the rhythm of Mamet's dialogue going before you go there. I think Joe Mantegna once said that improv is not the order to the day when performing Mamet, so it's ironic how often the style is suggested. Read *Glengarry Glen Ross* or *American Buffalo*…but if you're in a hurry a quick cheat is David Ives *Speed the Play*, a parody in the collection of his short plays *All in the Timing*. It's a comic synthesis of Mamet written for a tribute to the playwright. The Ives collection also has many wonderful pieces in it and is a must read for improvisers.

WILLIAMS – Immediately comment on how hot it is. Then there's a lot of sexual tension – a man being a brutish beast to women or a guy repressing his desire for another man – or perhaps a mother hoping to set her daughter up with a proper beau. And somehow it all seems to be set in or around New Orleans (or if the scene's already somewhere else then talk about taking a trip there) and how about something exotic for dinner? Iguana anyone?

As for movie styles that come up most often (the audiences we get seem too smart to give us "comedy"):

FILM NOIR – This is one of the rare times where it's okay, actually it's mandatory, for your spacework to produce an object out of thin air. As soon as the scene resumes in the film noir style, everyone onstage plucks a cigarette from nowhere and begins to smoke it. Also, the women in the scene are dames not to be trusted, everyone's striving for possession of some valuable dingus and the hero provides more narration of what's going on in the story than there is dialogue spoken between characters. The narration relies pretty heavily on simile and it is fun for one of the other characters to acknowledge they hear it. This happened in a memorable sketch on *Saturday Night Live* when Robert Mitchum was host and played a scene with Kevin

Nealon that parodied Mitchum's film work as private eye Philip Marlowe.

WESTERN – Bow your legs and hop around to insinuate the riding of horses. The central character in the scene stands alone against the villain with little hope of assistance from anyone else. There's some sort of duel that takes place. Being able to do a John Wayne impression is pretty handy (and a point well taken – your character can, when the style changes, start talking with a different accent or, in this case, twang).

In class we were doing a scene in a western style in which the sheriff was being told by the blacksmith that the lawman's horse had to be put down. My cousin Krystal and Carolyn, a student and member of the troupe, were playing the sheriff and blacksmith respectively. The stage was about 15 feet wide and they got to a point where the sheriff was so ticked-off at the blacksmith that she calls her out for a showdown in front of the saloon. So they got back-to-back in duel-like mode because...well, I guess they thought it was a French Western...and Carolyn's blacksmith said "all right then, twenty paces. Right?" and without missing a beat Krystal jumped right on Carolyn's line with "better make it seven." Very funny, because clearly there wasn't room in the actual physical space of the stage to walk off twenty paces, and impressive because of how fast Krystal processed that and got her line out.

SCI-FI – Suddenly the females have no idea what a kiss is but really want to know ('50s sci-fi). One of the cast members slips their hand beneath their shirt and starts trying to pop it through it at chest level (a la *Alien*). Or somehow one of the characters, in their best Charlton Heston voice, comes to realize that lunch is made of people - peeeee-puuuhhhhlllll! (*Soylent Green*). Perhaps everyone acts as if they are possessed by other-worldly forces (*Invasion of the Body Snatchers*) or the Tea Party.

WOODY ALLEN – This comes up a lot. The way to go is to play your character as the overly-philosophical nebbish who's obsessed with sex and death. Channel your inner-*Annie Hall* parody here.

As I mentioned earlier, the caller usually does not get involved in the scene. The exceptions for us have occurred when the playwright style has stumped the cast. Once we got Eugene O'Neill and the students looked lost, so the caller did a quick bit about delivering a block of ice. Another time, Sam Shepard was given. The performers were playing a couple, so the caller began acting as if he were an old man sipping liquor from a fruit jar full while commenting aloud about his romantic liaisons with the female character, his daughter.

49. SPIN ROTATION

The performers rotate through a scene while changing their dialogue when a bell rings.

We start with two performers onstage. The instructor serves as host and will be ringing a hotel call-bell during the scene. This type of bell can be purchased at an office-supply store.

Before discussing how we use the bell, I will discuss the technical aspects of how the performers are run through the scene.

The host asks for a relationship that the two students onstage could *reasonably* have. There's a reason for qualifying the relationship as "reasonable." We once did back-to-back shows with two men starting the scene and each time a good-time Charlie in the crowd called out the suggestion of "sisters."

The host repeats the suggestion to the audience. Let's say it is "co-workers." The host explains the game along these lines: "We're now going to play a scene for you between co-workers. Whenever I ring this bell, the performer who just spoke must change the last thing they said and change it as many times as the bell rings. The only thing that counts as the scene goes forward is the last thing they said. We take you to a scene between co-workers."

The performers consider how to use the suggestion and eventually one signals to the other that they will initiate. The scene begins.

At some point a third person comes onstage. As with any scene where someone enters, this performer must quickly establish who their character is. In this form, they also need to make it clear which of the two performers already onstage should leave by making a statement which makes it a natural choice for one of the performers to exit. If they want "Kurt" out of the scene, they might enter saying "Kurt, they're towing your car. You'd better get out there."

The person entering must always take charge because their entrance brings the audience's focus to them. The audience wants to know who they are and so do their scene partners.

The performer who leaves the stage justifies their departure; they explain why they are leaving. This first person to depart has a unique role in that they will return to the scene as the last person to enter. This brings the scene full circle. Everyone else, once they depart the scene, will not be coming back.

After the first person departs, the question of who departs when the next person enters is actually settled. The next performer into the scene must continue with the person who came in ahead of them. The other performer departs and their work is done – they will not return to the scene. By following this order, each performer will work onstage with two different performers for extended periods.

You must minimize the amount of time that there are three people onstage! Someone arrives. We find out who they are. The person who is supposed to go justifies why they are leaving and splits. The two remaining people carry the story forward.

The form continues this way until everyone has gone, with the last person to enter being that performer who was the first person to depart. They get to return because they only worked with one scene partner for an extended period – the person they started the scene with. Their return brings the scene full circle and completes the rotation of the performers.

Now let's discuss how the bell is used during the course of the scene.

During the scene, whenever the host rings the bell, the person who spoke last has to change the last thing they said. They have to change it as many times as the bell rings. I call the process of the bell ringing and the student changing what they have said "spinning." You've just said something, then the bell rings and so you have to replace a word in your sentence with a different word. Free your mind and let your internal Vanna spin your "word wheel" and whatever pops into your head is what you use. Just say it. Don't worry about what it "means."

The only thing that counts as the scene moves forward is the last thing said. Using the bell makes for a livelier scene. It's a challenge for the performers to justify, that is, make sense of, why they just ended up saying what they've said. It's fun for the audience as they get to see how they work their way out of things.

When the bell rings you don't want to radically change the last thing said. Usually you are just changing one aspect of the sentence. It's more effective this way because it allows the audience to better follow what's going on.

Your character says "I like your shirt" and the bell rings. The ideal sequence for changing things is:

"I like your shirt."
(BELL RINGS)

"I like your smile."

(BELL RINGS)

"I like your attitude."

Notice that the nature of the statement changes significantly each time even though only one word is being changed. This type of spinning is preferable to:

"I like your shirt."

(BELL RINGS)

"I like your pants."

(BELL RINGS)

"I like your shoes."

I prefer the first group of changes because things change so differently. In the latter, all that's being changed is types of apparel. It's typical for the latter sequence to occur when you are getting the hang of the game. It still works in the play of the game, so don't fret if you are not changing things dramatically – you will with practice. What must be avoided is:

"I like your shirt."

(BELL RINGS)

"My feet are killing me."

(BELL RINGS)

"The sun is shining brightly."

There are too many things changing. You run the risk of confusing the audience. They may not be able to follow what's going on. Also, it doesn't play well. It is the slightly-changing spinning that gets the strongest response.

Also, avoid just stating the one word you are changing:

"I like your shirt."
(BELL RINGS)
"smile"
(BELL RINGS)
"attitude."

Changing just one word will work, but it's better to try and repeat the full sentence leading up to the change. Like most anything, there are exceptions to this suggestion. I know that Dave is very adept at spinning. When the opportunity arises I often end up ringing the bell up to ten times on a single sentence. He will, as he senses what's going on, just keep changing the one word. The rat-a-tat results work quite effectively, although it goes against the general rule. Keep in mind one of the caveats of this book – everything is a suggestion, so feel free to adapt to what work bests for you.

Other technique tips:

- Arriving performers must quickly establish themselves. If the location requires that they knock before entering it's a big help because you can go thru the "knock-knock, who's there?" routine and basically announce yourself. Don't force the knock-knock! If the location is outdoors or a storefront business (e.g., dry cleaners, pizzeria) where you just walk in, then knocking to enter is going to look absurd to the audience.

- When the bell rings and a change is made, let the person make sense of the last thing they said by following it up with at least one more statement before the other performer speaks. It's often easier for that other person to make sense of the odd thing that ends up being said. Resist the impulse. It's a bigger payoff for the first person to make sense of what they've just said. If you have given them a chance to justify it and they cannot do so, then you have the right to help make sense of it. Just don't jump the gun. (This skill is also critical to form #51, The Written Word, page 251.)

- The departing person does not just take a hike. They have to make it clear why they are leaving – they need to justify their departure. Consider how there might be multiple points of access to the location. Just because everyone seems to be entering the scene from a certain spot does not mean that there cannot be other exits/entrances for the location. If the location is pizzeria and people are entering the scene thru the "front door" there can also be a hall leading to the bathrooms, or a staircase leading down to a basement storage area or one leading up to a second-floor apartment.
- Keep in mind that just because *the actor* knows that they will not return to the scene does not preclude *the character* they are playing from suggesting that they are stepping out for just a second but will be right back. (Another example of the actor/character duality kicking in.)
- The performers waiting to enter should stand together offstage. It's okay if the audience sees them. It is important that the performers see what is being established by the spacework. It

also helps the first person departing keep track of who has entered before they make their return at the end.

- Characters entering should know the characters they are continuing the scene with. It's the same rule of thumb as with other scene work. Avoid playing strangers.

- The bell can be rung to change physical actions and not just lines of dialogue. If someone sneezes, ring the bell. What do they change it to – a cough? – and ring again to see what else they can change it to – maybe the wheezing gasp you remember from the person sitting next to you on this morning's commute to work.

- A fun bit of business is for someone in the scene to break character and threaten to take the bell from the ringer and smash it if they keep getting "rung up." So, of course, the host rings the bell so that the nature of the threats keeps changing.

- When and how many times do you ring the bell? Knowing when to ring the bell is a skill unto itself. You try to ring the bell just often enough so that the performer is going to be challenged in justifying what they ended up saying. A good barometer is how the audience reacts. Leave them laughing is a good stand-up comic mantra. It applies here too. Don't beat it to death. If you ring three or four times and the responses are great, let it go. In a performance troupe, it's good to get everyone a shot at developing the skill of when to ring the bell. Before performance time you really want to home in on who is good at it. IF everyone seems reasonably adept, or equally inept, one variation in the play of the game is that each departing person takes over the bell-ringing duties; this allows the initial host/bell ringer to take part in the scene work.

- The scene will end shortly after the return of the first person to depart. The bell ringer picks a good moment to ring the bell rapid-fire, which cues the lights to blackout. This rapid-fire ringing can occur after a person has changed something after the bell's been rung or it can just spontaneously be tossed in after a well-received line is spoken.

One of the best pieces of advice I can give to nascent improv troupes is that you DO NOT have to take an audience's suggestion.

When we first started performing this improv we would simply ask for "a relationship the two students could have." I've already mentioned the "sisters" problem, where one night we had two men onstage and the suggestion from the audience was "sisters." They took it. The very next show the same scenario – two men onstage – and we get "sisters" again. That's when I changed it to "a relationship the two students could *reasonably* have."

This seemed to fix the problem. Then one night we had Liza and Michael onstage. Liza's an excellent improviser and always dressed nicely for performance; she had a light-colored blouse and black slacks on that night. So they ask for their relationship and got back "incestuous." I'm thinking they should have made like Manute Bol and forcefully rejected that one, but they took it.

So they began as a brother and sister and things got predictably icky in short order. Liza was doing a great improv by making it clear her character was not down with this deal. The bell was not helping much either, taking things from strange to bizarre.

After they had the story up and running, Jason Gordon (see page 11), an original student and troupe member, entered. As the first new person entering the scene, he had to make it clear who should go. It was Michael who had to go because Jason, establishing himself as their father, made it clear he wants to talk things over with Liza's character. Liza made her discomfort with "dad" clear, moving downstage and taking a seat there. Jason joined Liza downstage, sitting beside her.

"Why the long face?" he asks.

The bell rang and Jason immediately changes the line to...

"Why the long pants?"

One of the many great responses Jason's work got. This also just goes to prove that sometimes a suggestion that you probably should reject can work out and turn into something special.

50. ULTIMATE JEOPARDY!

This improv lampoons the motifs of the classic game show by bringing together the regular, celebrity and college champions.

A performer sets three chairs beside each other onstage and asks the audience for three suggestions: a living celebrity, a profession and something you might major in at college. These inputs are the basis for the characters to be played by the three contestants. The performer concludes by repeating the suggestions back to the audience and telling the audience "we take you to America's favorite quiz show."

The offstage announcer ("Johnny") gets things started by introducing the game and the contestants. By the time the announcer begins his introductions the three players have figured out who's doing what. Let's say that the inputs were Tom Cruise, dentist and biology. The announcer usually introduces players in order of who's weakest to who's strongest at playing the form. When the contestants arrive onstage following their introduction, and they should not be seen until it's completed, they should stand behind the chair – it serves as the contestant's podium, not a seat – and they should fill in the spots from furthest away from the host to closest, so that the best player is next to the host when starting. This is important for the end of the game.

Our announcer begins the festivities with: "This is the *Ultimate Jeopardy! Championship* and here are tonight's contestants. Our first challenger is our celebrity *Jeopardy!* champion. When he's not jumping on Oprah's couch, he's making blockbuster movies and little Scientologists, please welcome Tom Cruise." And the performer enters. We don't let anyone go onstage during their intro, because the non-celebrity contestants' last names are intended as jokes.

Give the regular and college champs a hometown and college, respectively, and you use their real first name. Make up a last name based on their assignment. Either the announcer comes up with these or, preferably, the performers make a choice and tell the announcer.

So, the announcer continues: "Our next contestant is our regular *Jeopardy!* Champion, she's a dentist from Austin, Texas. Please welcome Michelle Drill."

Then the announcer introduces the last player: "Our final contestant tonight is our college *Jeopardy!* Champion. She's a biology major from Holy Cross College, please welcome Mary Scott Intelligentdesign."

Then the host is introduced. It can be someone doing an Alex Trebek impersonation, or it can be any celebrity the host mimics well, the conceit being they are the guest host while Alex undergoes an emergency moustache graft.

ANNOUNCER: "And here's the host of *Jeopardy!* Alex Trebek."

"Trebek" enters as host. The announcer's duties are finished.

Our faux Trebek explains to the audience how things are going to work.

Host: "Good evening, ladies and gentlemen, I'm Alex Trebek and I'm Canadian. Welcome to *Jeopardy!* the show where you provide the answers and our contestants come up with the questions. To get things started tonight, we need three categories you might see on *Jeopardy!*"

The audience gives three categories. Let's say they are "Colors," "Presidents" and "Iran."

When selecting categories, leave out the dollar values unless it's agreed in advance that you'll start at $100 and with each subsequent selection go up $100 in value. You prepare this way so you don't end up asking twice for "Colors for $200," but, trust me; it's okay to skip the dollars.

The host announces that the player standing at the middle podium won the backstage drawing and gets to go first.

MIDDLE-PODIUM CONTESTANT: "I'll take Presidents, Alex."

The host then prompts the audience to provide an answer by saying "Presidents, the answer is..."

Hopefully at least one person in the audience will say a president's name. Let's say you get "Polk." Alex repeats "Polk!" to the audience to make sure everyone's heard it. In categories where you get a full name, the host should just give the last name back to the audience. It helps the performers to do their thing if they only have to deal with a single word.

And just what is that thing they must do? After selecting a category and getting the answer, if someone has a response, they need to "buzz in." This is done by miming the pressing of an imaginary buzzer on the podium and actually saying "buzz!" Then they give their response in the form of a question. The response takes things in a different direction entirely. Often, the best choice is a really bad pun, where you take the answer and since it sounds like something else, you make believe that's what was said and your question is the response to that.

Huh?

Well if the category is "Colors" and the answer is "mauve" – well, mauve sounds like Maude and so the response question could be "Who was played on TV by Bea Arthur?"

Another vein of response plays off some trivia associated with the answer. If the "Presidents" category elicits "Lincoln" a possible response is "Who's good for a $5 loan?" or "Who's the guy that dug that tunnel?" the latter playing better in NYC say, than Seattle.

Yet another avenue of response is the social commentary. If the category selected is "Iran" and the answer is "Ahmadinejad" the pejorative response can be "WHO SUCKS!?!"

The kind of response you generally want to avoid is the one that's based on your character. If the answer is "Brad Pitt" and the dentist is responding "Who would I really like to get in my dentist's chair" it might get an okay response but it's not the best way to go. If you must do so, try to keep what I call a self-referencing response to one per round. By the same token, even though the improv is about coming up with these jokey responses, it is okay to bring out your character assignments in the way in which you interact with each other.

Another type of response to avoid is the literally true, but not funny, response. If you're responding to the "Lincoln" answer with "Who was our 16th President?" Then you'd better be ready to hear the host say "True, but not funny."

The host controls the flow of the game. When a reply is given and it gets any kind of response from the audience, our host wants to move things right along to the next selection. Once someone has buzzed in and replied, it's okay for one, or, may the gods forbid, both of the other players to also chime in with a response. But they'd better be doing so because they have something better than the one before. Instructor! Be on guard for the performer who always thinks they've got something better to add and is invariably mistaken in that belief. It's your job to break the news to them.

An odd corollary to this: a player who is aces at this form can get things started with great replies to the first couple of selections, but should not overshadow their fellow players. Even if your next response would kill, give the other players a chance to chime in with something and let the game move on. A nice balance of all contestants replying will be most effective overall for the form. Good teamwork makes everyone shine.

Bits of in-game business:

- if one of the three contestants is not feeling the vibe and provides nothing while the game progresses, the host can call a timeout. The host steps over to their podium to check if their "buzzer" is still working by pressing the imaginary buzzer; then they make a buzzy sound them self, and exclaim "oh yes, it does seem to be working."

- if nobody has a response but the host can provide one, then he or she can advise the players that time's run out and the answer they were looking for is...and the host provides a response. The host should not do this more than once in any game.

- if nobody has anything, then someone should buzz in and ask if they can buy a vowel – wrong game, it's *Jeopardy!* not *Wheel of Fortune* – but it will move things along to the next choice.

- the host is more than welcome to comment on the quality of the responses which get a tepid reaction from the audience. It's also the host's job to affirm what they deem to be a correct response. They usually say

"Correct! You have control of the board. Please select a category."

After about eight or so selections, it's time to move on, so our host moves the game to *Final Jeopardy!* Preferably this occurs when things are on a roll, after a couple of really clever contestant responses, so that your audience is left wanting more.

ALEX (following response to the last "answer"): "And that takes us to *Final Jeopardy!* The scores are close enough (even if someone's been dominating) that this will determine tonight's champion. Tonight's final category is "*Men's Names*" and in that category, the final answer is..." (The final category is always determined prior to the show and known to all the players. We often use either "Men" or "Women's" names or nicknames.) The audience gives the answer, let's say it's "Ralph." Alex repeats it to the audience and then says: "Our contestants will write down their questions to the answer "Ralph" while we hum the *Jeopardy!* theme (the *THINK* music written by *Jeopardy!* creator Merv Griffin).

The humming of the theme was a pretty straightforward proposition when we were first beginning to perform, but one night, Kevin, our non-pareil host, decided it would be a good thing to have the audience hum as if they were drunk. Great idea! In subsequent shows he had the audience humming the theme as if angry, French, sad, etc. For all your improvisations, take time to really think about how they work and what you can change, or what you can add, to enhance them. Give it a try in rehearsal to see if it will work. Don't spring it out of nowhere during a show. The good instructor will embrace and employ clever modifications.

When the humming concludes, our host says: "Thank you studio audience. The category is *"Men's Names"* and the answer is "Ralph." We'll reveal all three responses before deciding if any are funny." Then he quickly says the name of the player farthest away from him and adds "the answer is Ralph."

The player farthest away just has to say their question. "What did I do all weekend after eating that warm mayonnaise?" The next player is listening to hear if that reply is similar to what they planned to say. If not, they simply fire away, but if it is they have to use the second reply they prepared "Who sends Alice to the moon?" The third player is also listening and may have to go with their third reply. Perhaps it's "What does, let's face it, Joseph Fiennes call his brother when they're alone?" That's why positioning the best player closest to the host is key — they have to come up with three possible replies in case the people going ahead of them do something similar first — we don't want repeats!

Based on who gets the biggest response, our host proclaims them the winner and concludes with a big "See you next time on *Jeopardy!*" to the audience.

Keep in mind that this is one of those stand-alone improvisations. You are not creating a scene, so what you do in it, as the contestant, can be a little more profane, scatological or naughty than you should strive for in a scene-based form. So if the category is "James Bond Villains" and the "answer" is "Oddjob," feel free to respond "What do you get from a gal with way too many collagen injections?" Still and all, clever is best, even goofy-clever like the Maude answer above, so try not to resort to frat-boy humor.

51. WRITTEN WORD

Performers act a scene inspired by a historic event, interspersing in their dialogue statements which were written by the audience on slips of paper.

This form also makes a great performance piece. It is so good that it's usually our finale when we're not doing *Strip Charades* (page 257.) It's a particularly good finale for a small performing group (five or fewer people).

Three performers are onstage. The form can also be done with two students but three makes for more energy and is a greater challenge to pull off.

Before the show begins have the audience write simple declarative sentences on slips of paper. Place them in a bowl or hat and keep it onstage throughout the performance so that the audience sees they have not been tampered with.

When it comes time for this form, each performer takes three slips of paper from the bowl. As they pass it from one to the other, they take turns in explaining how the game works.

FIRST PERFORMER: "Earlier this evening we asked you to write sentences on these slips of paper."

SECOND PERFORMER: "We'll each take three sentences and use them during the course of the scene, trying to justify them when we do so."

THIRD PERFORMER: ""But to begin the improv, we need from you the suggestion of a historic event."

Hold the sentences in your hand! I've seen many performers tuck their sentences into their pockets only to "lose" them when they want to read one. You hold them in your hand and, after reading one, let it drop to the floor. The time it takes to hit the floor buys you some time to think about how to justify why you just said that seemingly random phrase.

Using the suggestion of historic event, one of the three students will initiate the scene with spacework. The other two players should both be in the scene from the start and should be doing their own spacework. Within the first half minute after dialogue begins, it should be clear who the characters are to one another, where they are and what is going on in the context of the historic event. Then the performers can get into the game of the scene, which is reading the sentences.

There's no pre-set order for reading the sentences. Each performer should read one sentence before anyone reads their second sentence. This first round becomes the order in which the players will read their remaining sentences. Stick to this order!

When a performer decides it's time to work in a sentence, it's important that they make a big production out of it. You really want to make the audience aware that you are about to read one of "their" sentences and you want it to be crystal clear where your words end and their written words begin.

Also – and I cannot stress how important it is for this to be embraced by the performer – the sentence that you read aloud is something your character is saying, believing, thinking or writing. You must take ownership of the sentence and not act as though it is something someone else said to you. Why? If the words are someone else's, then you can simply explain them away as the thoughts of someone a few slices short of a pizza. When they are your words, you have to justify! You have to explain why your character just said that.

If the instructor thinks the actors are not history whizzes you can substitute "reason to celebrate" for "historic event." This is not an improvement, however. It is fun for the audience to see what the actors make of a suggestion they're unsure of. For example, once we had three performers onstage and the suggestion was "Battle of Gettysburg." Now it's pretty sad that not one of the three knew it was the American Civil War battle of 1863. However, it was pretty funny that the scene they created revolved around their fighting the Getty Company's attempt to monopolize the gas stations in their city – their burg, if you will.

Tina Fey, creator and star of NBC-TV's hilarious multi-Emmy winning TV show, *30 Rock*, was interviewed for *Entertainment Weekly* in April, 2007. She was quoted as saying that she had a hard time reconciling how her show being watched by six million people was cause for disappointment when she could remember doing stage shows in Chicago for an audience of 2. I can identify with that, having done more than our share of performances before spare crowds. Since this form requires there be a minimum number of sentences in the bowl (three for each person in the scene), when I saw that the audience was small, I would write sentences and add them to the bowl to make sure that we had enough.

One recurring phrase I liked to write was "My first love was an insecure Arab girl." I don't know what possessed me to come up with that one (and it was the original title of this book), but it was selected for use in the show. It got such a response that whenever I had to write sentences I would jot it down and toss it into the bowl. The cast got so conditioned to its appearance that there was often an onstage reaction to it.

Sometimes you get the suggestion of an historic event which is open to interpretation. When the audience calls out Civil War, you know that they are expecting the *American* Civil War. It's fine to do the American Civil War. On more than one occasion though, I've done a scene as Picasso painting Guernica during the *Spanish* Civil War.

Pace is important. Establish the who/what/where of the scene during the first half minute and then start in with the sentences. Don't allow long pauses to occur before the next sentence is read. And remember to justify why your character just said what was written on that slip of paper. Another important rule is for the other two performers to give the person who's just read a sentence a chance to make the justification. Don't just plow into the next bit of dialogue. The justification you come up with can be just as funny, if not funnier, than the reaction to the sentence being read.

Because the performers will stick to an order for reading the sentences, the person running the lights should be able to keep track and know when the last sentence is coming. This way they can black out the lights just as soon as it is read. So although the final sentence won't have to be justified, it makes for a nice button, or finish, to the form.

What if the lights don't go out when they should? Continue the scene for a bit and then very deliberately pick one of the used sentences off the floor and re-use it, all the while staring intently in the direction of your lighting operator. The lights will go off after that.

52. STRIP CHARADES

This is a performance piece where a cast member has to guess a sentence created by the audience. Plus stripping.

Although the entire troupe is involved in this dilly, there are two main players: the one who has to guess the phrase and the person who plays the main scene with them and helps guide them along.

A cast member is introduced by a performer onstage who then sends them out of the room to the "isolation booth." The performer then asks the audience to make up a sentence – something totally original, not a cliché or proverb. Then they use words like these to inform the audience what is going to happen:

"I'll be playing a scene with the returning cast member. This scene will be interrupted by the rest of the cast, who will first perform a scene inspired by the entire phrase and, subsequently, perform scenes giving clues to the individual words in the phrase. The improvisation is over when the cast member guesses the phrase word for word." Just as the performer is about to let the other performer back into the room, they let the audience know "After the first scene, every time a minute goes by, I will remove something I'm wearing. "

Yikes!

When the performer brings the person outside back in, they initiate a scene which is somehow vaguely inspired by the phrase. The performer is not trying to give a direct clue to the phrase. It's just a basis for getting started.

Eventually their scene will be interrupted by other cast members who come onstage to perform a clue-giving scene. The original two performers simply observe.

The first clue-giving scene is intended as an all-encompassing representation of the phrase. (A rule for all these clue-giving scenes is that you cannot say any of the key words from the phrase.) After the scene the performer takes a stab at the phrase. I'm always encouraging them to be "big and proud," which means to be loud and energetic, whenever making these guesses. A nice bit of business, after the initial guess, is to say "That's it! Good night everyone!" but you plow on.

The subsequent clue-giving scenes are for a specific word or two of the sentence.

The clues can be for the words of the sentence in any random order. They do not have to be in sequence.

For the best effect, the first clues should be for words that *sound* like the words in the sentence. Once the guesser gets the sound-alike word, the stripping performer helps them understand that it is a sound-alike by simply telling them "Yes! and the word in our phrase sounds like that one."

The charm that you strive for within the playing of the game is that the clue-giving scenes should be good scenes in their own right. They should not seem to exist solely for getting across the word you're trying to clue the guesser in on. Always avoid the trap of playing what I call a "trivia answer" or "fill in the blank" scenes because it is completely without charm. For example if "heart" is the word you're trying to relay to the guesser, it's not really much fun to have a scene where someone meets Celine Dion and keeps on asking "Hey Celine, I loved the movie *Titanic* but c'mon, does *IT* really go on? Does *IT*? I mean, *IT* can't really GO ON, can *IT*?" A better tact, if you're hell bent on going the *Titanic* route, would be to play Jack and Rose swimming near the headboard and **eventually** she's confessing how hers is going to go on but Jack's is about to stop.

When the clue-giving scenes begin, the guesser does not start spewing out guesses whenever they want. When the performers playing the scene think they've done enough, they will prompt the guess to be made. Usually, the scene stops and one of the players turns to the guesser, breaks character (stops playing their character) and says something along the lines of "You know what this scene's about!," "You know what's going on here!," "You know what his problem is!" and so on.

If the performer guesses correctly, that's great. If, however, they are wrong, then maybe the players of the scene might do a little bit more, but a better choice is for them to tuck their tails between their legs and skulk offstage. Whether you do a brief reprise or depart, you don't want to stay out there and try and drag the right guess out of the guesser. That won't "play," which is to say that the audience won't enjoy it.

Once we were playing the game and I was leading Jay, who was the guesser. "Dance" was a word in our phrase. So they played a scene in which Santa was being told by two reindeer that a certain colleague – "No Santa. Not Dasher, Comet, Cupid or Blitzen." – has gotten himself trashed again and won't be able to make the Christmas Eve run. It was a great scene and an excellent choice for how to go after "dance" by getting him to guess "Dancer." However, Jay, two-time winner of NYC's funniest amateur *Jewish* comedian competition, had absolutely no idea what the reindeer names are. The players were frustrated because they did this well-received scene but he was clearly not going to get it. They had forgotten that it does not matter if he gets it as long as they have done a good scene. Well, maybe it mattered a bit to me as I'd soon be standing onstage in my drawers, but I think you get the point. As soon as I sensed the players were trying to talk their way into getting Jay to guess it, I dismissed them from the stage with "For God's sake, he was raised in an Orthodox household, get off the stage." and that's what the person in my role has got to do – move things along. We want to see the next clever scene, not a bunch of performers trying to drag the right guess out of someone.

Don't worry, I'll get to talking about how you manage the stripping, which is, of course, completely optional, but let me cover some other tips first.

When going for the small words – an "a," or "the" you really get a chance to be clever, but you can also have a set-piece handy to knock them off. When we were first starting, if we needed someone to guess "the" we would play a scene set at the local video store (this was long before NetFlix) where customers were asking the counterperson if they could check their system for the movie title they wanted. Thing was, they always seemed to leave one word out, so the clerk couldn't help them.

"Yeah, uh, do you have *Dark Knight, Guns of Navarone* or *Magnificent Seven?*"

Then the next person asking would be worse.

"Have you got that musical *Fiddler on Roof?*

...and they wouldn't even use a Russian accent.

Fine. Not the cleverest way to get "the" but it helped get the job done and kept me from getting arrested for indecency. Yes, it does contravene my wanting to avoid "fill in the blank" clues, but we're talking about the small words here. Beware, though, because it can develop an almost Pavlovian response in the guesser. You remember Pavlov – he would ring a bell before feeding his dogs, and then once he'd been doing it for a while, he'd ring the bell without feeding them and they'd be salivating wondering where the heck lunch was.

Anyway, we were playing the game one night and the cast had to get the guesser to guess "my." So they started the video store scene and people were asking things like "Do you have that musical *Fair Lady?*" or "Have you got that TV series *So Called Life?*" and the guesser turns to me and says, in a bored manner, "the." I almost got down to the jock strap that night.

The person stripping has to manage the flow of the form. When the clue given is a sound alike word, they alert the player. When the word you need is "dance" and they've been given "dancer," the stripper tells the guesser how much they hate the letter R, that it should be banned – in other words, delete R from the word given. The stripper also has to keep the words of the phrase in order, especially since the clues can come in any order. As a rule of thumb, every time a clue is given, whether the guesser gets it or not, the stripper should go over which words they have gotten to that point.

Which brings us to the stripping. Why? Well, I'd say why not, but let's not make it a blue state versus red state thing. The reason is to make the form more engaging for the audience by raising the stakes. Without the stripping, the form can get a bit monotonous as we work the sentence out with the guesser.

I swear that we're working to make sure that the student stripping does not go the full Monty. Much as I tried over the years to get Jen, Linda or Alexa to do the stripping, it was always me doing the undressin' and believe me, I'm much more Chip & Dale than Chippendale.

You really want to put some funny jokes into it. First off, I have about 14-15 things on. I don't say that every time a minute goes by I'll remove "an article of clothing"; rather I say "something I'm wearing" so that my watch, a necklace, or Band-Aids over nipples can be removed and buy me another minute. Also, I try to make it clear that it's something coming off *every minute after the first clue is given*, which means after the first clue-giving scene is performed. For some reason, the person calling the time (usually the one running our light board) always seemed to make it every minute from when the guesser returns to the stage. Bastard!

Somewhere beneath the initial layer of jacket, sweater, shirt and undershirt is my bra – my flaming red, velvety and not all that supportive bra. Yes, it's a very Uncle Miltie (Google Milton Berle, kids) moment to be standing onstage in your bra, but it always gets a reaction; mostly positive. Though we have had some walkouts over the years, by men insecure in either their own sexuality or jealous of my fashion sense.

Usually when I'm down to my undershirt, if I know we've got a way to go, when the next minute is called to cue me to strip, I'll first drop my pants and show off whatever hideous boxers I have on before I take the undershirt off and show the bra.

A typical costuming for me – and I've got this on throughout the entire gosh darn show – is:

Kangol cap (turned backwards, Sam Jackson style)
Shark-tooth necklace (retired from my regular wardrobe by my wife)
Jacket
Sweater
Polo Shirt (horse not croc)
Belt
Pants
Shoes
Socks
Watch
Bracelet or thick rubber band
Boxer shorts
Second pair of boxer shorts
Tighty whities (A *Risky Business* homage)
A jock strap

Maybe a second jock strap if I think that night's guesser is not that good a guesser

Band-Aids over each nipple – though white hospital tape is more visually striking

One white tube sock rolled up so that it's about a 6 inch tube

Since we never get past the boxers (the jock strap is more a safety precaution), the last thing that's pulled out, very dramatically and usually at the resolution of the phrase, is the tube sock which has been secreted in/about the tighty-whities. It's always provides a good, cheap laugh. (If you are the one stripping, some feigned anxiety is always good. Just make sure that the cast knows that you're acting.)

It's important that the performers backstage maintain some discipline. The sentence should be written on a piece of paper and the words you've gotten should be checked off. They must keep their voices down as they figure out who's doing what next. You don't want to overshadow the work going on onstage. Also, be supportive of one another. If someone has an idea and needs you to play the scene with them, go for it, even when you're not completely sure what their idea is.

When you get the phrase – and you will get the phrase – thank your audience and bring the cast out so they can tell everyone who they are and take bows.

Whether in class or performance, have fun with your improvisations and keep the energy high.

Thanks for your purchase of this book. For additional info, please be sure to check my website, www.gsimprov.com. I will be posting additional content there, including improvs not included in this book. I look forward to getting your feedback about the book there and to hear about your improv adventures.

APPENDIX A: Recommended Reading and Viewing

I recommend these books:

Making Movies by Sidney Lumet is a great text by the legendary director. A simply wonderful book.

Improv Comedy by Andy Goldberg is a fine introductory book which I found very helpful when I started.

Truth in Comedy by Close, Halpern, and Johnson is an excellent book for improvisers who already have some training under their belt.

A Challenge for the Actor by Uta Hagen. This is the renowned teacher's preferred text. She also wrote *Respect for Acting*.

Audition by Michael Shurtleff reminds us why 'keeping the stakes high' is a must.

Sanford Meisner on Acting by Sanford Meisner and Dennis Longwell covers the prominent acting technique, which I also find to be much attuned with improv.

Impro for Storytellers by Keith Johnstone. I think this one "reads" more easily than the better known *Impro*.

Improvisation for the Theater by Viola Spolin is the bible of improv.

How To Be a Working Actor by Henry & Rogers is a good practical text. I met these ladies at a Learning Annex session in NYC and it was a great presentation.

All In The Timing, Fourteen Plays by David Ives. Fantastic; especially *Sure Thing, The Universal Language* and *Speed the Play*, which is the quintessential David Mamet parody.

Of course, an improviser should also be listening to music. I enjoy the witty lyrics of *Bowling for Soup* and *Pink*. Music can inspire your creativity. For example, a perfect meeting of artistry and commercial needs is Chris Cornell's *You Know My Name*. It's the theme song for *Casino Royale*, the first James Bond film with Daniel Craig. It's a great piece of work in the way it links what we know about James Bond to the film's story.

Here are my must-see movies, which are great grist for your improv mill, as riffing off great movies comes up time and again in improv:

Western: *The Searchers, My Darling Clementine, The Westerner, High Noon, The Outlaw Josey Wales, The Magnificent Seven, Unforgiven, Dances with Wolves*

Comedy: *Animal House, Bronco Billy* (an underrated film and one of the great screwball comedies), *The Hot*

Rock, *The Lavender Hill Mob, The Pink Panther, Catch Me If You Can, The Naked Gun, Midnight Run, Airplane, Top Secret, Annie Hall*

Sci-Fi: *The Matrix, Aliens, Soylent Green, Planet of the Apes (Heston), Omega Man (Heston)*

Musical: *Oklahoma!, West Side Story, Sound of Music, Phantom of the Opera, Chicago*

Film Noir: *The Third Man* (my favorite film, with a great ending fadeout which Scorcese paid homage to in *The Departed*), *Maltese Falcon, The Big Sleep (Bogart), Chinatown, The Hot Spot, Red Rock West*

Sports: *Hoosiers, Rocky & Rocky Balboa, Rudy, Field of Dreams, Tin Cup*

Romance: *Casablanca* (the greatest film of all time), *When Harry Met Sally, The Ghost and Mrs. Muir, The Way We Were, To Catch a Thief*

Gangster: *The Godfather Trilogy* (yes, I even like the third one), *Casino, Goodfellas, The Departed*

Courtroom: *The Verdict, Anatomy of a Murder, To Kill a Mockingbird*

War: *Saving Private Ryan, The Dirty Dozen, Paths of Glory, Sands of Iwo Jima, From Here to Eternity, Braveheart*

Classics: *Lawrence of Arabia, Lust for Life, The Ten Commandments* (awesome and almost comically over-the-top), *Ben Hur, North by Northwest, It's A Wonderful Life, Citizen Kane, Raiders of the Lost Ark*

Animation: *Toy Story 1-3, Aladdin, Snow White, The Simpsons Movie, Shrek 1-4*

Others: *Bad Day at Black Rock, Suddenly, The Manchurian Candidate* (Sinatra), *The Quiller Memorandum, Pan's Labyrinth, Amelie, Airport, Elmer Gantry, The Fugitive*

Films about Actors: *Living in Oblivion, Tootsie, Shakespeare in Love, All About Eve, Galaxy Quest*

Bond, James Bond: *Goldfinger, Casino Royale, Dr. No, Moonraker*

And a lot more I'll wish I had included about a week from now.

APPENDIX B: Finding the Right Class

Here are some thoughts, originally posted on my gsimprov.com website, about what to consider when you are in the market for an improv class; or any acting class.

Always ask if you can take a free audit (observe-only) or pay for a single trial class. This way you can see how the teacher teaches and what the mix is of your potential classmates. Even if there's only one class available locally, it's no fun to sign up for a class that makes you miserable because it's not right for you.

Is the teacher prepared? If the teacher has a game plan for each class you are probably in good hands. A performing teacher is a plus because they are "in the mix" - still active and enthused about improv. They can relate practical information to about what works in a performance. Try to find out what training they have.

It seems like a small thing, but it really is important: is the teacher consistently on time? If the teacher starts late, do they extend the ending time of the class?

The teacher should make you and your fellow students always feel comfortable, both physically and socially. The class space should be clean and easily accessible. A teacher who makes their students feel comfortable is just as important. When I first started teaching, I thought charging $5 a class would help me build a following. It did, but I later found out from one of my better students why she held off on coming to the class for a couple of years. She figured that if the class was that cheap I must just be some guy on the make, so I schtupped her. Just kidding.

The instructor should be able to give you clear, concise instruction. You will also want feedback on your work. Is the feedback positive? Is it consistent? Does the teacher allow questions from the student?

The price of the class should be clear. ASK! Also ask about the refund or credit policy in case you have to drop the class or miss a class. Ask if everyone in the class pays the same rate. Some classes offer returning students a steep discount – this is often a practical necessity but don't be shy about asking.

Ask if the teacher teaches all the classes. Beware classes where the teacher is substituted for a lot or where the occasional sub seems unqualified.

Check out the teacher and/or school online. By the same token, keep in mind that anybody can put up a website or make a posting, so if you see a good or bad notice, consider the source.

If the teacher is an independent, avoid anyone who seems motivated more by separating you from your money than a true passion for teaching. Ask them how long they have been teaching – there's no substitute for experience, but not having a lot of it does not necessarily mean that they won't be a good teacher. There were only about eight students in Uta Hagen's first class, but Jack Lemmon was one of them. Especially with an independent, ask if you can pay-as-you-go for a while before paying it all up front. Perhaps you can pay for a month's worth of classes before paying for an entire semester.

Beware "phony" classes - ones that exist to push other services on you (e.g., headshots, spiritual enlightenment). Class should be about learning improv - everything else is beside the point.

Who are the students in the class? A class with a healthy mix of returning students and "new blood" is ideal. Always try and audit a class - you get to see how the teacher teaches and if the students are sharing or competitive.

Good students help make for good teachers - be considerate of your fellow students. Be a sharing person, follow the teacher's guidelines and you will do your part to help make the class a great experience.

Visit www.gsimprov.com for improv news and updates.

Follow us on twitter @GSIMPROV.

Made in the USA
Charleston, SC
26 February 2011